# Modern Web Design in 30 Days

Beginner's Guide to HTML, CSS & JavaScript with Projects, Exercises, and AI-Powered Learning

**Laurence Lars Svekis**

<packt>

# Modern Web Design in 30 Days



**Portfolio Director:** Ashwin Nair
**Relationship Lead:** Nitin Nainani
**Project Manager:** Ruvika Rao
**Content Engineer:** Hayden Edwards
**Technical Editor:** Arjun Varma
**Indexer:** Hemangini Bari
**Production Designer:** Deepak Chavan
**Growth Lead**: Anamika Singh

First published: March 2026

Production reference: 1150426

Published by Packt Publishing Ltd.

Grosvenor House

11 St Paul's Square

Birmingham

B3 1RB, UK.

ISBN 978-1-80760-449-3
www.packtpub.com

*For Alexis and Sebastian*

*Thank you for your support*

# About the author

**Laurence Lars Svekis** is a web developer, instructor, and educator who focuses on teaching web technologies through practical learning and real coding examples. He has created numerous tutorials, courses, and educational resources that help learners understand how modern websites are built. His teaching style emphasizes hands-on practice so that learners develop confidence while working with HTML, CSS, and JavaScript. By breaking down complex topics into clear explanations, he helps beginners build strong foundations in web development. Through his online training platforms and learning resources, Laurence has supported thousands of students worldwide in developing programming skills and understanding modern web technologies.

# Table of Contents

# Preface

Modern Web Design in 30 Days introduces the core technologies behind modern websites through a structured and approachable learning journey. Designed for beginners, the book guides readers through the tools used to build web pages while encouraging a practical, hands-on learning process.

The journey begins with the foundations of how the web works, explaining how browsers interpret HTML, CSS, and JavaScript to display and control pages. Readers learn to structure content with semantic HTML, apply visual styling with CSS, and add interactivity using JavaScript.

As the chapters progress, the book explores layout techniques such as Flexbox and CSS Grid, responsive design for different screen sizes, and principles that improve usability and visual clarity. Readers gain insight into how websites organize content, structure layouts, and guide user interaction.

Each chapter encourages experimentation, allowing readers to modify code, test ideas, and observe results. The book also introduces AI-assisted prompts that help reinforce understanding and support deeper exploration of key concepts.

By the end of the 30-day journey, readers will understand how modern websites are structured, styled, and enhanced with interactive features, providing a solid foundation for further study in web development.

## Who this book is for

This book is for beginners who want to learn how modern websites are built using HTML, CSS, and JavaScript. It is ideal for students, aspiring developers, and designers who want to understand the technical side of web creation.

The structured 30-day format makes it especially helpful for self-learners looking for a clear path to build practical web development skills from the ground up.

## Download the example code files

The code bundle for the book is hosted on GitHub at `https://github.com/lsvekis/Modern-Web-Design-in-30-Days`.

For more content from the author, visit `https://basescripts.com/`.

# Get in touch

Feedback from our readers is always welcome.

**General feedback**: If you have questions about any aspect of this book or have any general feedback, please email us at `customercare@packt.com` and mention the book's title in the subject of your message.

**Errata**: Although we have taken every care to ensure the accuracy of our content, mistakes do happen. If you have found a mistake in this book, we would be grateful if you reported this to us. Please visit `http://www.packt.com/submit-errata`, click **Submit Errata**, and fill in the form.

**Piracy**: If you come across any illegal copies of our works in any form on the internet, we would be grateful if you would provide us with the location address or website name. Please contact us at `copyright@packt.com` with a link to the material.

**If you are interested in becoming an author**: If there is a topic that you have expertise in and you are interested in either writing or contributing to a book, please visit `http://authors.packt.com/`.

# 1

# What Is Web Design & How the Web Really Works

**Day 1 of 30**

## Learning Objectives (What You Will Be Able to Do)

By the end of this chapter, you will be able to:

- Clearly explain what web design is and what it is not
- Describe the roles of HTML, CSS, and JavaScript in a website
- Explain how a website loads in a browser at a high level
- Identify structure, style, and interaction on real websites
- Use browser tools to inspect a website's building blocks
- Begin thinking like a designer–developer, not just a user

These objectives focus on **understanding,** not memorization.

## Vibe Learning Mindset (Chapter Focus)

"Before you write code, you must understand the system."

This chapter builds **mental models** — the foundation for everything you'll learn next.

# 1. What Is Web Design?

Web design is the practice of creating experiences for the web.

It combines:

- Communication
- Problem solving
- Visual hierarchy
- Technical implementation

A website is not just "content on a screen." It is an **interactive environment** designed for people.

## Web Design vs Web Development

| Web Design | Web Development |
|---|---|
| User-focused | Logic-focused |
| Visual hierarchy | Functionality |
| Layout & flow | Data & behavior |
| Experience-driven | Rule-driven |

Modern web designers often do *both*.

## Example: A Simple Blog Page

Think about a blog article:

- The title and paragraphs → HTML
- The font, spacing, and colors → CSS
- The like button or comments loading → JavaScript

All three layers work together.

# 2. The Three Core Layers of the Web (Deeper Understanding)

## HTML — The Structure Layer

HTML answers:

- What content exists?
- What type of content is this?

Examples:

- Is this text a heading or a paragraph?
- Is this image decorative or informative?
- Is this a button or just styled text?

HTML is about **meaning**, not appearance.

## CSS — The Presentation Layer

CSS answers:

- How should this content look?
- How should it be arranged?

CSS controls:

- Visual hierarchy
- Spacing and alignment
- Color and contrast
- Responsiveness across devices

CSS tells the browser *how to present meaning*.

## JavaScript — The Behavior Layer

JavaScript answers:

- What happens when the user interacts?
- How should the page respond?

Examples:

- Clicking a button
- Submitting a form
- Updating content without reloading
- Animations and transitions

JavaScript introduces **decision-making**.

# 3. How a Website Loads (Step-by-Step Mental Model)

Let's slow this down.

- User action — You enter a URL
- Browser request — The browser asks a server for files
- Server response — HTML, CSS, JS files are sent
- Browser rendering:
- HTML creates structure
- CSS styles it
- JavaScript adds logic

The browser is constantly interpreting instructions.

## Example Analogy: A Restaurant

- HTML → Menu items
- CSS → Plate presentation
- JavaScript → Ordering, payments, interactions

# 4. Learning Object 1 — Identify Web Layers in the Wild

## Exercise 1 — Website Breakdown

Choose **two different websites:**

- One content-heavy (news, blog)
- One interactive (app, dashboard)

For each site, list:

- HTML elements you can identify
- CSS design patterns
- JavaScript interactions

### Exercise 2 — Screenshot & Annotate

Take a screenshot of a webpage and:

- Label structure areas
- Highlight design choices
- Mark interactive elements

## 5. Learning Object 2 — Exploring the Browser Tools

### Exercise 3 — Inspecting HTML

- Open any website
- Right-click → Inspect
- Expand HTML elements
- Notice:
- Nesting
- Tag names
- Structure

### Exercise 4 — Live Style Changes

In DevTools:

- Change a color
- Adjust font size
- Toggle a layout rule

Observe changes instantly.

You are editing a live website locally.

# 6. Learning Object 3 — Thinking Like a Web Designer

## Exercise 5 — Design Intent

Pick a homepage and answer:

- What is the main goal?
- What do they want you to do first?
- How do colors guide attention?

### Exercise 6 — UX Awareness

List:

- One thing that feels intuitive
- One thing that feels confusing

# AI-Assisted Learning Prompts (Expanded)

## Prompt 1 — Mental Model Reinforcement

"Explain HTML, CSS, and JavaScript using a real-world analogy I haven't heard before."

## Prompt 2 — Contrast Learning

"Show me what a website would feel like without JavaScript."

## Prompt 3 — Guided Curiosity

"What are common beginner misunderstandings about web design?"

## Prompt 4 — Reflection Support

"Ask me 5 reflective questions to help me understand web design better."

# 7. Learning Object 4 — Mini Experiments (Low Risk)

## Exercise 7 — Breaking & Fixing (Conceptual)

Imagine:

- Removing all CSS from a site
- Removing all JavaScript

- Removing all HTML

Describe what would remain.

### Exercise 8 — Role Swap

Explain web design:

- To a non-technical friend
- To a business owner
- To a designer

Each explanation should change.

## Knowledge Check (Expanded Quiz)

### Question 1

Why is HTML considered semantic?

A) It controls design

B) It defines meaning

C) It adds logic

D) It styles text

**Correct: B**

HTML describes what content is, not how it looks.

### Question 2

Which layer controls responsiveness?

A) HTML

B) CSS

C) JavaScript

D) Server

**Correct: B**

CSS adapts layouts to different screens.

## Question 3

Why is JavaScript optional but powerful?

A) Browsers don't support it

B) It replaces CSS

C) It enhances interaction

D) It stores data

**Correct: C**

## Reflection & Learning Log

Write short answers:

- What part of web design surprised you?
- What part feels most approachable?
- What part feels unclear (for now)?

Confusion is a signal — not a failure.

## Vibe Learning Wrap-Up

Today you:

Built a mental map of the web

Learned how websites actually work

Observed real systems

Practiced reflective thinking

Tomorrow, you'll **write your first HTML page**.

## Day 2 Preview

**Your First Website: Writing HTML from Scratch**

You'll move from observer to creator.

# 2

# Your First Website: Writing HTML from Scratch

**Day 2 of 30**

## Learning Objectives

By the end of this chapter, you will be able to:

- Create a working HTML page from scratch using the core page structure
- Explain what <!doctype html>, <html>, <head>, and <body> do
- Use essential HTML elements: headings, paragraphs, links, images, lists
- Use attributes correctly (href, src, alt, title, lang, etc.)
- Organize content with basic semantic structure (even before CSS)
- Debug common beginner HTML mistakes confidently
- Use AI prompts to extend learning (without outsourcing understanding)

## Vibe Learning Mindset (Chapter Focus)

"Make something real, fast. Then improve it."

You'll build a real page today—then you'll **experiment, break it, fix it, and understand it.**

# What You're Building Today

A simple personal "starter homepage" that includes:

- A title and intro
- A few sections (About, Skills, Links)
- An image
- A list
- A link that opens in a new tab

By the end of Day 2, you'll have a complete HTML file you can keep improving all month.

## 1. What Is HTML (Really)?

HTML stands for **HyperText Markup Language**. It is not a programming language.

HTML is a **markup language**—it "marks up" content with meaning.

- A heading is marked as a heading (<h1>)
- A paragraph is marked as a paragraph (<p>)
- A link is marked as a link (<a>)

The browser reads HTML and builds a **DOM** (Document Object Model)—a structured tree of elements.

HTML is the structure layer: it defines what exists and what it *is*.

## 2. The Minimal HTML Page (Your Foundation)

Every HTML page starts with the same core skeleton:

```
<!doctype html>
<html lang="en">
<head>
  <meta charset="utf8" />
  <meta name="viewport" content="width=devicewidth, initialscale=1" />
  <title>My First Website</title>
</head>
<body>
  <h1>Hello, web!</h1>
```

```
    <p>This is my first HTML page.</p>
  </body>
  </html>
```

## What Each Part Does

`<!doctype html>`

Tells the browser to use modern HTML standards (HTML5)

`<html lang="en">`

The root element of the page & lang helps accessibility tools and search engines

`<head>`

"Behind the scenes" info: page title, metadata, links to CSS, scripts (sometimes)

`<meta charset="utf8">`

Supports modern characters and symbols

`<meta name="viewport" ...>`

Makes the page behave properly on mobile screens

`<title>`

Shows in the browser tab and search results

`<body>`

Everything visible on the page lives here

# 3. Learning Object 1 — Build Your First File

## Exercise 1 — Create index.html

- Create a folder on your computer called: webdesignday2
- Create a file inside it called: index.html
- Paste the skeleton code above
- Open it in a browser (doubleclick the file)

You have a website.

# 4. Core HTML Elements You'll Use Constantly

## Headings

Headings create structure and hierarchy:

```
<h1>Main Title</h1>
<h2>Section Title</h2>
<h3>Subsection Title</h3>
```

**Rule:** Use headings in order (don't jump from `h1` to `h4` unless there's a reason).

## Paragraphs

```
<p>This is a paragraph of text.</p>
```

## Links (Anchor Tags)

```
<a href="https://example.com">Visit Example</a>
```

Open in new tab (optional):

```
<a href="https://example.com" target="_blank" rel="noopener">Visit
Example</a>
```

**Why add `rel="noopener"`?**

It's a security best practice when using `target="_blank"`.

## Images

```
<img src="photo.jpg" alt="A description of the image" />
```

**The `alt` attribute is required for accessibility** and helpful when images don't load.

## Lists

Unordered list (bullets):

```
<ul>
  <li>HTML</li>
  <li>CSS</li>
  <li>JavaScript</li>
</ul>
```

Ordered list (numbers):

```
<ol>
  <li>Plan</li>
  <li>Build</li>
  <li>Improve</li>
</ol>
```

## 5. Learning Object 2 — Build a Real Starter Homepage

Paste this into your <body> (replace content with yours):

```
<body>
  <header>
    <h1>My Web Design Journey</h1>
    <p>Hi! I'm learning how to build websites with HTML, CSS, and
JavaScript.</p>
  </header>
  <main>
    <section>
      <h2>About Me</h2>
      <p>
        I'm a beginner learning web design in 30 days. My goal is to build
and publish a real website.
      </p>
    </section>
    <section>
      <h2>What I'm Learning</h2>
      <ul>
        <li>HTML – structure</li>
        <li>CSS – design</li>
        <li>JavaScript – interaction</li>
      </ul>
    </section>
    <section>
      <h2>My Links</h2>
      <p>
        One site that inspires me is
        <a href="https://developer.mozilla.org/" target="_blank"
```

```
rel="noopener">MDN Web Docs</a>.
      </p>
    </section>
    <section>
      <h2>Image</h2>
      <p>Add an image file to your folder and reference it below.</p>
      <img src="myimage.jpg" alt="A personal or placeholder image for my
homepage" />
    </section>
  </main>
  <footer>
    <p>Made on Day 2 of my Web Design in 30 Days challenge.</p>
  </footer>
</body>
```

## Why This Structure Matters

You just used semantic building blocks:

- <header> for the top content
- <main> for the primary content
- <section> for grouped ideas
- <footer> for page ending

Even without CSS, your page is already organized and meaningful.

## 6. Learning Object 3 — Debugging Like a Builder

HTML is sensitive to structure. Common mistakes:

### Mistake 1 — Forgetting closing tags

```
<p>This paragraph never closes...
```

Fix:

```
<p>This paragraph closes.</p>
```

### Mistake 2 — Incorrect nesting

Bad:

```
<p><h2>Title</h2></p>
```

Fix:

```
<h2>Title</h2>
<p>Text</p>
```

### Mistake 3 — Broken image path

If your image doesn't show:

- Is the filename correct?
- Is it in the same folder?
- Did you use the correct extension?

Quick test:

Try replacing with a known online image URL (for testing only).

## 7. MicroExperiments (Vibe Learning Core)

### Exercise 2 — Change One Thing at a Time

Make one change, refresh, observe.

Try:

- Change the <title> and see browser tab update
- Add a new section
- Add a second link
- Add a second list

The fastest learners run tiny experiments.

### Exercise 3 — "Break It On Purpose"

Do each of these and then fix it:

Remove a closing tag

Change <h1> to <h3>

Delete the alt attribute

Put a <p> inside an <a> and see what happens

Write down what you noticed.

# AI Prompts (Chapter 2)

## Prompt 1 — Explain My Code

```
"Here is my HTML. Explain what each section does and suggest improvements
for semantics."
```

## Prompt 2 — Idea Generation

```
"Give me 5 ideas for beginner websites I can build in the next 30 days,
based on my interests."
```

## Prompt 3 — Debugging Helper

```
"My image isn't showing. Ask me the most likely questions to diagnose the
issue."
```

## Prompt 4 — Accessibility Check

```
"Review my HTML for accessibility problems and recommend improvements."
```

# Mini Project (End of Chapter)

## Exercise 4 — "About Page Upgrade"

Add:

- A "Goals" section using an ordered list
- A "Contact" section with at least 2 links (email + website)

Example:

```
<section>
  <h2>Goals</h2>
  <ol>
    <li>Build a clean homepage</li>
    <li>Style it with CSS</li>
    <li>Add interactivity with JavaScript</li>
  </ol>
</section>
<section>
  <h2>Contact</h2>
  <p>
    Email: <a href="mailto:hello@example.com">hello@example.com</a><br />
```

```
    Website: <a href="https://example.com" target="_blank"
rel="noopener">example.com</a>
  </p>
</section>
```

# Knowledge Check (Quiz + Explanations)

## Q1: What belongs inside <head> ?

A) Headings and paragraphs

B) Visible content

C) Metadata and page settings

D) Buttons and images

**Answer: C**

`<head>` contains information *about* the page.

## Q2: Why is alt important?

A) It makes images load faster

B) It helps accessibility and fallback descriptions

C) It changes image size

D) It adds animation

**Answer: B**

## Q3: Which is a semantic element?

A) `<div>`

B) `<section>`

C) `<span>`

D) `<br>`

**Answer: B**

Semantic elements describe meaning and structure.

## Reflection (Vibe Learning)

Answer:

What felt easy today?

What felt confusing?

What part of your page do you want to improve tomorrow?

## Chapter WrapUp

Today you:

Built your first real HTML webpage

Used core elements and attributes

Practiced semantics and structure

Learned to debug with experimentation

## Day 3 Preview

**Text, Links, Images, and Page Structure (More HTML Depth)**

You'll make your content richer and more "real website" ready.

# 3

# Text, Links, Images & Page Structure

**Day 3 of 30**

## Learning Objectives

By the end of this chapter, you will be able to:

- Structure written content clearly using headings and text elements
- Use links correctly for navigation, external sites, and actions
- Add and manage images properly in a webpage
- Understand and apply basic semantic page structure
- Improve readability, accessibility, and clarity of content
- Think intentionally about how users read web pages
- Use AI prompts to refine content structure and clarity

## Vibe Learning Mindset (Chapter Focus)

"Good web design starts with clear communication."

Before colors, layouts, or animations — **content and structure come first.**

This chapter teaches you how to:

- Organize ideas
- Guide attention
- Make pages readable and usable

## What You're Building Today

You'll **upgrade your starter homepage** into a more complete, readable, and structured page by:

- Improving text hierarchy
- Adding meaningful links
- Managing images correctly
- Using semantic layout elements intentionally

## 1. How People Read on the Web

Users do not read websites line by line.

They:

- Scan headings
- Skim paragraphs
- Look for links and visuals
- Decide quickly whether to stay or leave

Your job as a web designer is to **guide the eye.**

### Visual Hierarchy (Without CSS Yet)

Even with plain HTML, you control hierarchy by using:

- Headings (h1–h3)
- Paragraph spacing
- Lists
- Section grouping

HTML alone already communicates structure.

## 2. Headings: Your Page's Skeleton

### Heading Levels and Meaning

```
<h1>Main Page Title</h1>
<h2>Major Section</h2>
<h3>Subsection</h3>
```

Rules to remember:

- One `<h1>` per page
- Headings should be meaningful
- Don't use headings just to make text "big"

## Exercise 1 — Improve Heading Structure

Look at your current page:

- Do sections have clear titles?
- Are headings ordered logically?

Refactor if needed.

# 3. Paragraphs, Line Breaks & Emphasis

## Paragraphs

```
<p>This is a paragraph of text.</p>
```

Keep paragraphs short:

- 2–4 sentences max
- One idea per paragraph

## Emphasis

```
<strong>Important text</strong>
<em>Emphasized text</em>
```

**`<strong>`** → importance

**`<em>`** → emphasis

These are **semantic**, not visual.

## Line Breaks (Use Sparingly)

```
<br />
```

Use `<p>` instead of stacking `<br>` tags.

## 4. Links: Navigation & Actions

Links are the **core of the web.**

### Basic Link

```
<a href="https://example.com">Visit Example</a>
```

### Opening in a New Tab

```
<a href="https://example.com" target="_blank" rel="noopener">
  Visit Example
</a>
```

### Email Link

```
<a href="mailto:hello@example.com">Email Me</a>
```

### Common Beginner Mistake

❌ "Click here"

Use descriptive text:

```
<a href="https://example.com">Read the full documentation</a>
```

### Exercise 2 — Improve Your Links

Replace vague link text

- Add at least:
- One external link
- One email link

## 5. Images: Meaningful, Not Decorative

Images can:

- Support content
- Guide attention
- Build emotional connection

They should never be random.

### Basic Image Tag

```
<img src="photo.jpg" alt="A description of the image" />
```

Rules:

- alt is required
- Describe the image's purpose
- Be concise but clear

### Folder Organization (Best Practice)

```
webdesignday3/
│
├── index.html
└── images/
    └── profile.jpg
```

```
<img src="images/profile.jpg" alt="Portrait photo of me" />
```

### Exercise 3 — Image Audit

For each image on your page:

- Why is it there?
- What does it communicate?
- Is the alt text meaningful?

## 6. Semantic Page Structure (Expanded)

HTML provides elements that describe **purpose**, not appearance.

### Common Layout Structure

```
<header>Intro content</header>
<nav>Navigation links</nav>
<main>Main content</main>
<section>Grouped content</section>
<article>Independent content</article>
<footer>Closing info</footer>
```

## Example: Improved Page Layout

```
<body>
  <header>
    <h1>My Web Design Journey</h1>
    <p>Learning modern web design step by step.</p>
  </header>
  <nav>
    <a href="#about">About</a> |
    <a href="#learning">Learning</a> |
    <a href="#contact">Contact</a>
  </nav>
  <main>
    <section id="about">
      <h2>About Me</h2>
      <p>I'm learning web design in 30 days.</p>
    </section>
    <section id="learning">
      <h2>What I'm Learning</h2>
      <ul>
        <li>HTML structure</li>
        <li>CSS design</li>
        <li>JavaScript interaction</li>
      </ul>
    </section>
  </main>
  <footer>
    <p>Day 3 – Modern Web Design for Beginners</p>
  </footer>
</body>
```

# 7. Learning Object — User Flow Thinking

## Exercise 4 — Reading Path

Ask yourself:

- What does the user read first?
- What should they notice next?
- Where should their eyes land last?

Reorder content if needed.

## 8. MicroExperiments (Vibe Learning Core)

### Exercise 5 — Small Changes, Big Impact

Try:

- Changing heading text
- Reordering sections
- Removing one paragraph entirely

Observe how clarity improves.

### Exercise 6 — Content Reduction

Cut **20% of your text.** Does the page become clearer?

## AI Prompts (Chapter 3)

### Prompt 1 — Content Clarity

```
"Rewrite this section of my webpage to be clearer and more
beginnerfriendly."
```

### Prompt 2 — Accessibility Review

```
"Review my HTML text, links, and images for accessibility improvements."
```

### Prompt 3 — UX Perspective

```
"How would a firsttime visitor experience this page?"
```

### Prompt 4 — Structural Suggestions

```
"Suggest better section organization for this webpage."
```

## Mini Project — Homepage Content Upgrade

### Exercise 7

Add:

- A <nav> section
- Section IDs for navigation
- At least one internal anchor link

Example:

```
<a href="#contact">Jump to Contact</a>
```

## Knowledge Check (Quiz + Explanations)

### Q1: Why use semantic elements?

A) They make pages load faster

B) They improve meaning, accessibility, and structure

C) They replace CSS

D) They add interactivity

Answer: B

### Q2: What makes good link text?

A) Short and vague

B) Styled with CSS

C) Descriptive and meaningful

D) Hidden

Answer: C

### Q3: Why avoid long paragraphs on the web?

A) Browsers limit text length

B) Users skim instead of read

C) HTML can't handle long text

D) CSS breaks

Answer: B

## Reflection (Vibe Learning)

Answer:

How did structuring content change your page?

What felt easier today than yesterday?

What still feels uncertain?

## Chapter WrapUp

Today you:

Improved content clarity

Structured text intentionally

Used links and images correctly

Thought about users, not just code

## Day 4 Preview

Introduction to CSS: Making Your Website Look Like a Website

You'll finally style your page — without breaking its structure.

# 4

# Introduction to CSS: Making Your Website Look Like a Website

**Day 4 of 30**

## Learning Objectives

By the end of this chapter, you will be able to:

- Explain what CSS is and why it exists
- Connect CSS to an HTML file correctly
- Write basic CSS rules using selectors and properties
- Style text, colors, and backgrounds
- Understand how CSS rules are applied by the browser
- Use experimentation to refine visual design
- Use AI prompts to explore design improvements responsibly

## Vibe Learning Mindset (Chapter Focus)

"Separate structure from style."

HTML defines **what exists.**

CSS defines **how it looks.**

This separation is one of the most important ideas in web design.

## What You're Building Today

You'll transform your plain HTML page into a visually styled website by:

- Adding color
- Choosing fonts
- Improving spacing
- Making content easier to read

By the end of today, your site will **look intentional**.

## 1. What Is CSS (And Why It Exists)?

CSS stands for **Cascading Style Sheets**.

CSS was created because:

- Mixing content and design became messy
- Designers needed control over presentation
- Websites needed consistency across pages

Before CSS, styling lived inside HTML — which quickly became unmanageable.

### CSS Controls:

- Colors
- Fonts
- Spacing
- Layout
- Responsive behavior

CSS tells the browser *how to present* the HTML structure.

## 2. How CSS Works (Mental Model)

A CSS rule has three parts:

```
selector {
  property: value;
}
```

Example:

```
p {
  color: blue;
}
```

- Selector → What to style
- Property → What aspect to change
- Value → How to change it

### Exercise 1 — Read CSS Out Loud

Read this rule in plain English:

```
h1 {
  color: darkblue;
}
```

"Style all `h1` elements so their text color is dark blue."

## 3. Connecting CSS to HTML

### Step 1 — Create a CSS File

Create a new file:

```
styles.css
```

### Step 2 — Link CSS in HTML <head>

```
<link rel="stylesheet" href="styles.css" />
```

Place this **inside** `<head>`, not `<body>`.

### Exercise 2 — Test the Connection

Add this to `styles.css`:

```
body {
  backgroundcolor: #f5f5f5;
}
```

Refresh your page.

If the background changes, your CSS is connected.

# 4. Styling Text (Your First Design Tools)

## Font Basics

```
body {
  fontfamily: Arial, sansserif;
}
```

This creates a **font stack** — a fallback system.

## Font Size

```
p {
  fontsize: 16px;
}
```

## Text Color

```
p {
  color: #333;
}
```

## Exercise 3 — Improve Readability

Try:

- Changing font size
- Changing text color
- Applying styles to headings

Observe how readability changes.

# 5. Colors & Backgrounds

## Background Color

```
body {
  backgroundcolor: white;
}
```

## Section Backgrounds

```
section {
  backgroundcolor: #ffffff;
}
```

## Color Choices Matter

Good contrast improves:

- Readability
- Accessibility
- User comfort

If text is hard to read, the design has failed.

## Exercise 4 — Color Experiment

Try three different color schemes:

- Light background / dark text
- Dark background / light text
- Soft neutral palette

Which feels best?

# 6. Spacing: Margin & Padding (Critical Concept)

Spacing affects **everything**.

## Margin — Space outside an element

```
section {
  margin: 20px;
}
```

## Padding — Space inside an element

```
section {
  padding: 20px;
}
```

## Visual Difference

- Margin separates elements
- Padding creates breathing room inside elements

### Exercise 5 — Spacing Control

Add padding to:

a. Sections

b. Header

c. Footer

Notice how clarity improves.

## 7. Learning Object — Styling Your Page Step by Step

### Starter CSS Example

```
body {
  fontfamily: Arial, sansserif;
  backgroundcolor: #f4f4f4;
  color: #333;
  margin: 0;
}
header, main, footer {
  maxwidth: 800px;
  margin: auto;
  padding: 20px;
}
header {
  backgroundcolor: #ffffff;
}
footer {
  textalign: center;
  fontsize: 14px;
  color: #666;
}
```

Add this and tweak values slowly.

## 8. MicroExperiments (Vibe Learning Core)

### Exercise 6 — One Change Rule

Change only **one CSS property at a time.**

Ask:

- What changed?
- Why did it change?
- Was it better?

### Exercise 7 — Remove & Compare

Temporarily remove:

- All margins
- All padding
- All colors

Observe the difference.

## AI Prompts (Chapter 4)

### Prompt 1 — Design Feedback

```
"Review my CSS and suggest improvements for readability and clarity."
```

### Prompt 2 — Color Theory

```
"Suggest a beginnerfriendly color palette for a personal website."
```

### Prompt 3 — Debugging Helper

```
"Why might my CSS not be applying correctly?"
```

### Prompt 4 — Incremental Improvement

```
"What small CSS changes would have the biggest impact on user experience?"
```

## Mini Project — First Visual Upgrade

### Exercise 8

Create a simple style system:

- Background color
- Primary text color
- Heading color
- Spacing values

Write them at the top of your CSS as comments.

```
/*
Color palette:
Background: #f4f4f4
Text: #333
Accent: #2c7be5
*/
```

## Knowledge Check (Quiz + Explanations)

### Q1: What does CSS stand for?

A) Computer Style System

B) Cascading Style Sheets

C) Color Style Syntax

D) Creative Style Sheets

**Answer: B**

### Q2: Where should CSS be linked?

A) Inside `<body>`

B) Inside `<footer>`

C) Inside `<head>`

D) Inside `<main>`

**Answer: C**

### Q3: What is padding?

A) Space outside an element

B) Space inside an element

C) Font size

D) Border thickness

**Answer: B**

## Reflection (Vibe Learning)

Answer:

How did styling change how your site feels?

Which CSS property surprised you most?

What still feels unclear?

## Chapter WrapUp

Today you:

Connected CSS to HTML

Styled text and backgrounds

Controlled spacing

Learned to design with intention

## Day 5 Preview

### CSS Selectors & The Cascade: How Styles Are Applied

You'll learn *why* CSS behaves the way it does — and how to control it.

# 5

# CSS Selectors & the Cascade: How Styles Are Applied

**Day 5 of 30**

## Learning Objectives

By the end of this chapter, you will be able to:

- Explain what CSS selectors are and why they matter
- Use common selectors confidently (element, class, id)
- Understand how multiple CSS rules affect the same element
- Explain the idea of the CSS cascade in simple terms
- Predict which CSS rule will "win" in common situations
- Avoid common beginner mistakes with selectors
- Use AI prompts to diagnose and improve CSS behavior

## Vibe Learning Mindset (Chapter Focus)

"CSS is not random. It follows rules."

When beginners say *"CSS is broken"*, what they usually mean is:

"I don't understand which rule is being applied."

This chapter gives you **control**.

## What You're Building Today

You'll improve your existing styles by:

- Targeting specific elements more precisely
- Creating reusable styles
- Understanding why some styles override others

By the end of today, CSS will feel **predictable**, not magical.

## 1. What Is a CSS Selector?

A **selector** tells the browser **which HTML elements** a style rule should apply to.

Example:

```
p {
  color: blue;
}
```

This means:

"Select **all paragraph elements** and make the text blue."

### Read Selectors Like Sentences

CSS becomes easier when you read it out loud.

```
header p {
  color: green;
}
```

"Select paragraphs inside the header and make them green."

## 2. Element (Type) Selectors

The simplest selector targets **all elements of a type**.

```
h1 {
  color: darkblue;
}
p {
  font-size: 16px;
}
```

Use element selectors when:

- You want consistency
- You want a default style

## Exercise 1 — Element Selector Practice

Apply styles to:

- All paragraphs
- All headings
- All lists

Observe how quickly the site changes.

# 3. Class Selectors (Reusable Styling)

Classes allow you to style **specific elements**, not all of them.

## HTML

```
<p class="highlight">This paragraph is important.</p>
```

## CSS

```
.highlight {
  background-color: yellow;
}
```

**Keyrule:**

Class selectors start with a dot (.)

## Why Classes Matter

Classes let you:

a. Reuse styles
b. Avoid duplication
c. Stay flexible

## Exercise 2 — Create Reusable Classes

Create classes for:

a. Highlighted text

b. Card-like sections

c. Emphasis areas

Apply them to multiple elements.

## 4. ID Selectors (Unique Elements)

IDs are for **one unique element per page.**

### HTML

```
<section id="about">
  <h2>About Me</h2>
</section>
```

### CSS

```
#about {
  border: 2px solid #ccc;
}
```

**Key rules:**

a. IDs start with #

b. IDs must be unique

c. Use sparingly

### Exercise 3 — ID Usage

Add an ID to:

a. One main section

b. One special area

Style it differently from others.

## 5. Combining Selectors (More Control)

You can combine selectors to be more specific.

```
section p {
  line-height: 1.6;
}
```

"Select paragraphs inside sections."

## Another Example

```
header h1 {
  margin-bottom: 10px;
}
```

## Exercise 4 — Context Styling

Style:

- Paragraphs only inside <main>
- Links only inside <nav>

# 6. The Cascade (The Core Idea)

**Cascade** means:

When multiple rules apply, the browser decides which one wins.

CSS decisions are based on:

- Specificity
- Order
- Inheritance

# 7. Specificity (Who Wins?)

More specific selectors override less specific ones.

## Example

```
p {
  color: blue;
}
.highlight {
  color: red;
}
```

If a paragraph has the class `highlight`, it becomes **red**.

## Specificity Order (Simplified)

From weakest to strongest:

- Element selector (p)

- Class selector (.highlight)
- ID selector (#about)

### Exercise 5 — Predict the Outcome

Before refreshing, guess what color text will be.

Then test.

## 8. Order Matters (Last Rule Wins)

If selectors have equal specificity, the **last rule** applies.

```
p {
  color: blue;
}
p {
  color: green;
}
```

Result: **green**

### Exercise 6 — Order Experiment

Swap the order of rules and observe changes.

## 9. Inheritance (What Flows Down)

Some properties are inherited from parent elements.

Example:

```
body {
  font-family: Arial, sans-serif;
  color: #333;
}
```

Paragraphs and headings inherit these unless overridden.

### Not Everything Inherits

- Margins ❌
- Padding ❌
- Borders ❌

### Exercise 7 — Inheritance Test

Set:

- Font on body
- Color on main

Observe what inherits and what doesn't.

## 10. Common Beginner Mistakes (And Fixes)

### ❌ "My CSS Isn't Working"

Checklist:

- Is the selector correct?
- Is the file linked?
- Is another rule overriding it?
- Is there a typo?

### ❌ Overusing IDs

IDs are powerful — too powerful.

**Prefer classes for flexibility.**

### ❌ Styling Without Structure

If HTML is messy, CSS becomes painful.

## AI Prompts (Chapter 5)

### Prompt 1 — Debugging Help

```
"My CSS rule isn't applying. Ask me diagnostic questions to find the
issue."
```

### Prompt 2 — Selector Improvement

```
"Rewrite my CSS selectors to be cleaner and more maintainable."
```

### Prompt 3 — Learning Reinforcement

```
"Explain CSS specificity using a real-world analogy."
```

## Prompt 4 — Refactoring Support

```
"Which styles should be global and which should use classes?"
```

## Mini Project — CSS Cleanup & Control

### Exercise 8

Refactor your CSS:

- Replace unnecessary IDs with classes
- Group related rules
- Remove duplicate styles

Add comments explaining *why* each rule exists.

## Knowledge Check (Quiz + Explanations)

### Q1: Which selector is most specific?

A) `p`

B) `.card`

C) `#header`

D) `section p`

**Answer: C**

IDs are the most specific.

### Q2: If two rules have equal specificity, which applies?

A) The first

B) The last

C) The shortest

D) The browser default

**Answer: B**

## Q3: Which property is inherited?

A) Margin

B) Border

C) Font-family

D) Padding

**Answer: C**

## Reflection (Vibe Learning)

Answer:

- What part of CSS felt confusing before today?
- What now feels clearer?
- How will this change how you write CSS?

## Chapter Wrap-Up

Today you:

Learned how CSS targets elements

Understood specificity and order

Gained control over the cascade

Reduced “CSS frustration”

## Day 6 Preview

**CSS Box Model: Spacing, Borders & Visual Balance**

You’ll learn why spacing makes or breaks design — and how to master it.

# 6

# The CSS Box Model: Spacing, Borders & Visual Balance

**Day 6 of 30**

## Learning Objectives

By the end of this chapter, you will be able to:

- Explain the CSS box model clearly and confidently
- Identify the four parts of every element's box
- Control spacing using margin and padding intentionally
- Use borders to visualize and debug layouts
- Predict how size and spacing affect layout
- Avoid common spacingrelated beginner mistakes
- Use AI prompts to reason about layout and spacing decisions

## Vibe Learning Mindset (Chapter Focus)

"Spacing *is* design."

Most beginner layouts fail not because of colors or fonts —

but because of **poor spacing decisions.**

The box model is how the browser thinks about space.

## What You're Building Today

You'll improve the **visual balance and clarity** of your website by:

- Adding consistent spacing
- Creating separation between sections
- Understanding why elements take up the space they do

By the end of today, your page will feel **calmer and more intentional**.

## 1. Every HTML Element Is a Box

No matter what it is:

- Paragraph
- Heading
- Image
- Section
- Button

Every element is treated as a **rectangular box** by the browser.

### The Four Parts of the Box Model

From the inside out:

- Content — text or image
- Padding — space inside the element
- Border — outline around the element
- Margin — space outside the element

```
[ margin ]
  [ border ]
    [ padding ]
      [ content ]
```

You don't see the box — but the browser always does.

## 2. Padding: Space Inside the Element

Padding creates breathing room **inside** an element.

```
section {
```

```
  padding: 20px;
}
```

This pushes the content away from the border.

### Individual Padding Sides

```
paddingtop: 20px;
paddingright: 30px;
paddingbottom: 20px;
paddingleft: 30px;
```

### Shorthand Padding

```
padding: 20px;            /* all sides */
padding: 10px 20px;      /* top/bottom, left/right */
padding: 10px 20px 30px; /* top, left/right, bottom */
padding: 10px 20px 30px 40px; /* top, right, bottom, left */
```

### Exercise 1 — Padding Exploration

Add padding to:

- Sections
- Header
- Footer

Observe how content becomes more readable.

## 3. Margin: Space Outside the Element

Margins create space **between elements.**

```
section {
  marginbottom: 30px;
}
```

### Vertical Spacing Control

Margins are critical for:

a. Separating sections
b. Improving scanability
c. Creating rhythm

### Exercise 2 — Vertical Rhythm

Add margins between sections:

- Too little
- Too much
- Just right

Which feels best?

## 4. Borders: Seeing the Invisible

Borders help you **visualize the box**.

```
section {
  border: 1px solid #ddd;
}
```

Use borders temporarily to:

- Debug layouts
- Understand spacing
- See element boundaries

### Exercise 3 — Debug with Borders

Add borders to:

- Sections
- Header
- Main content

Then remove them once you understand the layout.

## 5. Width, Height & Box Sizing

### Default Behavior (Important!)

By default:

```
width = content only
```

Padding and border are **added on top**.

This can cause layout surprises.

## Example Problem

```
section {
  width: 300px;
  padding: 20px;
}
```

Actual size becomes **340px**.

# 6. Fixing the Problem: boxsizing

## Best Practice

```
* {
  boxsizing: borderbox;
}
```

Now: width = content + padding + border

This makes sizing **predictable**.

## Exercise 4 — Box Sizing Test

Add `boxsizing: borderbox` and:

Compare element widths

Notice easier layout control

# 7. Centering Content (Beginner Win)

## Center a Block Horizontally

```
main {
  maxwidth: 800px;
  margin: auto;
}
```

This:

- Limits line length
- Improves readability
- Centers the layout

### Exercise 5 — Content Centering

Apply centering to:

- Main content
- Cards or sections

Observe how the page feels more professional.

## 8. Common Box Model Mistakes

### ❌ Using <br> Instead of Margin

Bad:

```
<br><br><br>
```

Good:

```
section {
  marginbottom: 30px;
}
```

### ❌ Inconsistent Spacing

Random spacing creates visual chaos.

Design prefers consistency.

### ❌ Padding vs Margin Confusion

- Padding → internal space
- Margin → external space

## 9. Learning Object — Spacing System

### Exercise 6 — Create a Spacing Scale

Choose a base unit (e.g. 8px):

a. Small: 8px
b. Medium: 16px
c. Large: 32px

Use only these values throughout your CSS.

This creates **visual harmony**.

# 10. MicroExperiments (Vibe Learning Core)

## Exercise 7 — Remove All Spacing

Temporarily remove:

- All margins
- All padding

Then add them back slowly.

Notice how structure emerges.

## Exercise 8 — Compare Two Versions

Create:

- Version A: tight spacing
- Version B: generous spacing

Which is easier to read?

# AI Prompts (Chapter 6)

## Prompt 1 — Layout Diagnosis

```
“My page feels cramped. Suggest spacing improvements using the CSS box
model.”
```

## Prompt 2 — Visual Balance

```
“Review my layout spacing and recommend changes for better visual
balance.”
```

## Prompt 3 — Beginner Debugging

```
“Why does my element look bigger than the width I set?”
```

## Prompt 4 — Design Thinking

```
“How do professional designers think about spacing systems?”
```

# Mini Project — Spacing Upgrade

## Exercise 9

Refactor your CSS:

- Add consistent padding to sections
- Add vertical margin between sections
- Center your main content
- Use boxsizing: borderbox

Add comments explaining your choices.

# Knowledge Check (Quiz + Explanations)

## Q1: Which property controls space *inside* an element?

A) Margin

B) Padding

C) Border

D) Width

**Answer: B**

## Q2: What does boxsizing: borderbox do?

A) Removes padding

B) Removes margin

C) Makes width include padding and border

D) Centers elements

**Answer: C**

## Q3: Why are borders useful for beginners?

A) They improve design

B) They replace padding

C) They visualize layout boundaries

D) They reduce spacing

**Answer: C**

## Reflection (Vibe Learning)

Answer:

- How did spacing change how your site feels?
- Which spacing mistake did you notice in your own page?
- What spacing rule will you follow going forward?

## Chapter WrapUp

Today you:

Mastered the CSS box model

Controlled spacing intentionally

Debugged layouts visually

Improved readability and balance

## Day 7 Preview

### CSS Layout Basics: Display, Block vs Inline & Flow

You'll learn *why elements stack or sit side by side* — and how to control it.

# 7

# CSS Layout Basics: Display, Flow & Positioning

Day 7 of 30

## Learning Objectives

By the end of this chapter, you will be able to:

- Explain how elements naturally flow on a webpage
- Understand the difference between block, inline, and inlineblock elements
- Use the display property intentionally
- Predict how elements will stack or align
- Control basic layout behavior without advanced tools
- Debug common layout confusion
- Use AI prompts to reason about layout problems instead of guessing

## Vibe Learning Mindset (Chapter Focus)

"Layout issues are logic issues, not styling failures."

Before Flexbox and Grid, you must understand **normal document flow**.

This chapter gives you that mental model.

## What You're Building Today

You'll refine your page layout by:

- Understanding why elements stack vertically
- Controlling inline vs block behavior
- Creating simple horizontal layouts
- Preparing your HTML structure for modern layout systems

By the end of today, layouts will feel **predictable**, not mysterious.

## 1. Normal Document Flow (The Default Behavior)

By default, the browser lays out elements in **normal flow**:

- Block elements stack vertically
- Inline elements flow horizontally
- Content follows the order of HTML

HTML order matters.

### Example

```
<h1>Title</h1>
<p>Paragraph one</p>
<p>Paragraph two</p>
```

Result:

- Each element appears on a new line
- Order matches the HTML

## 2. BlockLevel Elements

Block elements:

- Start on a new line
- Take full width by default
- Stack vertically

Common block elements:

- <div>
- <section>

- <header>
- <main>
- <footer>
- <p>

## Block Example

```
section {
  background: #eee;
  marginbottom: 20px;
}
```

Each section takes up its own row.

## Exercise 1 — Block Observation

Inspect your page and list:

a. Which elements are blocklevel?

b. Which ones naturally stack?

# 3. Inline Elements

Inline elements:

- Do NOT start on a new line
- Take only as much width as needed
- Flow with text

Common inline elements:

a. <span>

b. <a>

c. <strong>

d. <em>

## Inline Example

```
<p>
  This is <strong>important</strong> text with a <a href="#">link</a>.
</p>
```

Everything stays on one line unless it wraps.

## Exercise 2 — Inline Awareness

Add multiple links inside a paragraph.

Observe how they flow with text.

# 4. InlineBlock Elements (The Hybrid)

`inlineblock` combines the best of both worlds:

- Sits inline
- Accepts width, height, margin, padding

## Example

```
.card {
  display: inlineblock;
  width: 200px;
  padding: 16px;
  margin: 10px;
  background: #fff;
}
```

## Exercise 3 — InlineBlock Cards

Create 2–3 `.card` elements and display them side by side.

# 5. The display Property (Your Layout Switch)

The `display` property changes how an element behaves.

Common values:

- block
- inline
- inlineblock
- none

## Example

```
nav a {
  display: inlineblock;
  marginright: 15px;
}
```

This turns links into layoutfriendly items.

## Exercise 4 — Display Experiments

Try changing:

- A paragraph to inline
- A link to block
- A section to inlineblock

Observe the results.

# 6. Hiding Elements (Without Deleting Them)

`display: none`

```
.hidden {
  display: none;
}
```

- Removes element from layout
- Takes up no space

## Exercise 5 — Toggle Visibility

Apply `display: none` to:

- An image
- A section

Then remove it.

# 7. Positioning Basics (Introduction)

Positioning changes **where** elements appear.

## Static (Default)

```
position: static;
```

This is normal flow.

## Relative Positioning

```
position: relative;
top: 10px;
left: 10px;
```

Moves element **relative to itself.**

### Exercise 6 — Gentle Positioning

Apply `position: relative` to a heading and move it slightly.

⚠ Do not use positioning to fix layout problems yet — you're learning it to understand *what not to do.*

## 8. Why Layouts Break (Common Beginner Issues)

### ✖ Expecting Inline Elements to Accept Width

Inline elements ignore `width` and `height`.

Fix:

```
display: inlineblock;
```

### ✖ Fighting the Flow

If layout feels hard:

Check HTML order

Check element display type

### ✖ Overusing position

Positioning is not layout — it's adjustment.

## 9. Learning Object — Flow Awareness

### Exercise 7 — HTML Order Test

Move sections up or down in HTML.

Refresh.

Observe how layout changes.

Layout follows structure.

## 10. MicroExperiments (Vibe Learning Core)

### Exercise 8 — Layout Predictions

Before refreshing the page:

- Predict what will happen
- Then test

Prediction improves intuition.

### Exercise 9 — Simplify

Remove:

- All custom display rules
- All positioning

Then rebuild layout slowly.

## AI Prompts (Chapter 7)

### Prompt 1 — Layout Explanation

```
"Explain why my elements are stacking vertically."
```

### Prompt 2 — Debugging Helper

```
"Which CSS display value should I use in this situation?"
```

### Prompt 3 — Mental Model

```
"Explain normal document flow with a realworld analogy."
```

### Prompt 4 — Beginner Mistakes

```
"What are common layout mistakes beginners make with CSS display?"
```

## Mini Project — Navigation Bar Layout

### Exercise 10

Create a simple horizontal nav:

```
<nav>
  <a href="#">Home</a>
  <a href="#">About</a>
  <a href="#">Contact</a>
</nav>
nav a {
  display: inlineblock;
  marginright: 20px;
}
```

Enhance spacing and clarity.

# Knowledge Check (Quiz + Explanations)

## Q1: Which elements stack vertically by default?

A) Inline

B) Block

C) Inlineblock

D) Hidden

**Answer: B**

## Q2: Why use inlineblock?

A) To hide elements

B) To center text

C) To allow sizing while staying inline

D) To remove spacing

**Answer: C**

## Q3: What controls layout order?

A) CSS only

B) JavaScript

C) HTML order

D) Browser defaults

**Answer: C**

# Reflection (Vibe Learning)

Answer:

- What layout behavior confused you before today?
- What now feels predictable?
- When would you not use positioning?

# Chapter WrapUp

Today you:

Learned normal document flow

Controlled element behavior with `display`

Built simple layouts

Prepared for modern CSS layout tools

# Day 8 Preview

### Flexbox Fundamentals: Designing OneDimensional Layouts

You'll finally get a modern layout system — and it will make sense because of what you learned today.

# 8

# Flexbox Fundamentals: Designing One-Dimensional Layouts

**Day 8 of 30**

## Learning Objectives

By the end of this chapter, you will be able to:

- Explain what Flexbox is and when to use it
- Understand the difference between a flex container and flex items
- Control layout direction using flexdirection
- Align items using justifycontent and alignitems
- Create simple horizontal and vertical layouts with Flexbox
- Debug common Flexbox confusion
- Use AI prompts to reason about layout alignment and spacing

## Vibe Learning Mindset (Chapter Focus)

"Flexbox solves layout problems — but only if you ask the right questions."

Flexbox is not about memorizing properties. It's about understanding **direction, alignment, and space.**

# What You're Building Today

You'll convert parts of your website layout into **Flexboxbased layouts**, including:

- A horizontal navigation bar
- A row of cards
- Centered content

By the end of today, layout alignment will feel **intentional and controllable.**

# 1. What Is Flexbox?

Flexbox (Flexible Box Layout) is a CSS layout system designed to:

- Align items easily
- Distribute space dynamically
- Adapt to different screen sizes

Flexbox works in **one direction at a time:**

- Row or
- Column

If your layout is onedimensional, Flexbox is your tool.

# 2. Flex Container vs Flex Items

Flexbox has two roles:

## Flex Container

The parent element where Flexbox is enabled.

```
.container {
  display: flex;
}
```

## Flex Items

The direct children of the flex container.

```
<div class="container">
  <div class="item">One</div>
  <div class="item">Two</div>
  <div class="item">Three</div>
</div>
```

Only **direct children** become flex items.

## Exercise 1 — Identify Flex Roles

In your layout:

- Which element is the container?
- Which are the items?

# 3. Main Axis vs Cross Axis (Critical Concept)

Flexbox always has two axes:

- Main axis → primary direction
- Cross axis → perpendicular direction

By default:

```
flexdirection: row;
```

- Main axis → horizontal
- Cross axis → vertical

## Visual Thinking

- justifycontent → aligns along the main axis
- alignitems → aligns along the cross axis

## Exercise 2 — Axis Awareness

Before writing CSS:

- Identify the main axis
- Identify the cross axis

# 4. flexdirection: Controlling Layout Direction

```
.container {
  display: flex;
  flexdirection: row;
}
```

Common values:

- row (default)
- column
- rowreverse
- columnreverse

## Exercise 3 — Direction Switch

Change a layout from:

- Horizontal → vertical
- Vertical → horizontal

Observe how alignment rules change.

# 5. Aligning Items with justifycontent

Controls alignment along the **main axis.**

```
justifycontent: flexstart;
justifycontent: center;
justifycontent: spacebetween;
justifycontent: spacearound;
justifycontent: spaceevenly;
```

## Example — Center Navigation

```
nav {
  display: flex;
  justifycontent: center;
}
```

## Exercise 4 — Alignment Practice

Try each `justifycontent` value.

Ask:

- What problem does this solve?
- When would I use it?

# 6. Aligning Items with alignitems

Controls alignment along the **cross axis**.

```
alignitems: stretch;
alignitems: center;
alignitems: flexstart;
alignitems: flexend;
```

## Example — Vertical Centering

```
.container {
  display: flex;
  alignitems: center;
}
```

## Exercise 5 — CrossAxis Control

Vertically center:

- Text inside a container
- Navigation links
- Cards

# 7. Flexbox in Real Layouts (Navigation Example)

## HTML

```
<nav class="nav">
  <a href="#">Home</a>
  <a href="#">About</a>
  <a href="#">Projects</a>
  <a href="#">Contact</a>
</nav>
```

## CSS

```
.nav {
  display: flex;
  justifycontent: spacebetween;
  alignitems: center;
}
```

Result:

- Horizontal layout
- Even spacing
- Clean alignment

## 8. Spacing with gap (Modern Best Practice)

Instead of margins:

```
.container {
  display: flex;
  gap: 20px;
}
```

Benefits:

- Cleaner code
- Consistent spacing
- Easier adjustments

### Exercise 6 — Replace Margins with Gap

Use gap instead of margin between flex items.

## 9. Common Flexbox Mistakes (And Fixes)

### ❌ Forgetting display: flex

If Flexbox isn't working — check this first.

### ❌ Mixing Up Axes

Remember:

- justifycontent ≠ always horizontal
- It follows the main axis

### ❌ Applying Flexbox to the Wrong Element

Flexbox goes on the **parent**, not the children.

# 10. Learning Object — Predict Before You Code

## Exercise 7 — Prediction Practice

Before refreshing:

- Predict alignment
- Then test

Prediction builds intuition faster than guessing.

# 11. MicroExperiments (Vibe Learning Core)

## Exercise 8 — Flex Layout Variations

Create:

- Leftaligned nav
- Centered nav
- Evenly spaced nav

Using **only Flexbox properties.**

## Exercise 9 — Column Layout

Convert a card layout from row → column.

# AI Prompts (Chapter 8)

## Prompt 1 — Flexbox Debugging

```
"My Flexbox layout isn't aligning correctly. Ask me questions to diagnose
it."
```

## Prompt 2 — Axis Explanation

```
"Explain main axis vs cross axis with a simple analogy."
```

## Prompt 3 — Layout Suggestion

```
"Is Flexbox the right choice for this layout? Why or why not?"
```

## Prompt 4 — Refactoring Help

```
"Refactor this layout to use Flexbox more cleanly."
```

# Mini Project — Flexbox Card Row

## Exercise 10

Create a card layout:

```
<div class="cards">
  <div class="card">HTML</div>
  <div class="card">CSS</div>
  <div class="card">JavaScript</div>
</div>
.cards {
  display: flex;
  gap: 20px;
}
.card {
  padding: 20px;
  background: #fff;
  border: 1px solid #ddd;
}
```

Experiment with:

- Alignment
- Direction
- Spacing

# Knowledge Check (Quiz + Explanations)

## Q1: What does Flexbox control?

A) Twodimensional layouts

B) Onedimensional layouts

C) Typography

D) Colors

**Answer: B**

## Q2: Which property aligns items along the main axis?

A) `alignitems`

B) `justifycontent`

C) `gap`

D) `flexwrap`

**Answer: B**

## Q3: Where does display: flex go?

A) On the child elements

B) On the parent container

C) In HTML

D) On the body only

**Answer: B**

# Reflection (Vibe Learning)

Answer:

- What Flexbox problem did this chapter solve for you?
- What still feels confusing?
- When would you not use Flexbox?

# Chapter WrapUp

Today you:

Learned Flexbox fundamentals

Controlled alignment and spacing

Built real layouts

Gained confidence in modern CSS

## Day 9 Preview

### Flexbox Advanced: Wrapping, Sizing & Responsive Behavior

You'll learn how Flexbox adapts to different screen sizes — and why it's so powerful.

# 9

# Flexbox Advanced: Wrapping, Sizing & Responsive Behavior

**Day 9 of 30**

## Learning Objectives

By the end of this chapter, you will be able to:

- Explain why responsive layouts are necessary
- Control wrapping behavior using flexwrap
- Use flex shorthand to size items intelligently
- Understand flexgrow, flexshrink, and flexbasis
- Build layouts that adapt to screen size changes
- Avoid common Flexbox responsiveness mistakes
- Use AI prompts to reason about responsive layout behavior

## Vibe Learning Mindset (Chapter Focus)

"Responsive design is not about devices — it's about flexibility."

Flexbox layouts respond to **available space**, not screen labels like "mobile" or "desktop."

## What You're Building Today

You'll upgrade your Flexbox layouts so they:

- Wrap naturally when space runs out
- Resize items proportionally
- Adapt gracefully to different viewport widths

By the end of today, your layouts will feel **fluid instead of fragile**.

## 1. Why Layouts Break on Small Screens

A layout that looks good on a wide screen can fail when:

- There isn't enough horizontal space
- Items are forced into one row
- Text becomes cramped

Flexbox solves this by allowing items to:

- Wrap
- Grow
- Shrink

## 2. Wrapping Flex Items with flexwrap

By default, Flexbox tries to keep everything on **one line**.

```
.container {
  display: flex;
  flexwrap: nowrap;
}
```

### Enable Wrapping

```
.container {
  display: flex;
  flexwrap: wrap;
}
```

Now items move to the next row when needed.

### Exercise 1 — Wrapping Experiment

Create a row of cards and:

- Resize the browser
- Observe when items wrap
- Notice how layout adapts

## 3. Combined Shorthand: flexflow

```
Instead of writing:
flexdirection: row;
flexwrap: wrap;
```

You can write:

```
flexflow: row wrap;
```

### Exercise 2 — FlexFlow Practice

Switch between:

- row nowrap
- row wrap
- column wrap

Observe behavior changes.

## 4. Flexible Sizing: The flex Property

The `flex` property controls how items grow, shrink, and size.

```
flex: grow shrink basis;
```

Example:

```
.card {
  flex: 1 1 200px;
}
```

### What This Means

- flexgrow: 1 → item can grow
- flexshrink: 1 → item can shrink
- flexbasis: 200px → starting size

## Exercise 3 — Size Control

Try:

- flex: 1
- flex: 2
- flex: 0 1 300px

Observe how space is distributed.

# 5. Understanding flexgrow

Controls how extra space is distributed.

```
.item {
  flexgrow: 1;
}
```

Two items:

- Item A → flexgrow: 1
- Item B → flexgrow: 2

Item B gets twice the extra space.

## Exercise 4 — Proportional Layout

Create:

- Sidebar (flexgrow: 1)
- Main content (flexgrow: 3)

Resize the window and observe balance.

# 6. Understanding flexshrink

Controls how items shrink **when space is limited**.

```
.item {
  flexshrink: 1;
}
```

Set:

flexshrink: 0 → item won't shrink

## Exercise 5 — Shrink Test

Prevent one card from shrinking while others adapt.

# 7. Understanding flexbasis

Defines the **starting size** before growth/shrink.

```
.card {
  flexbasis: 250px;
}
```

Combined with wrapping, this creates **responsive grids.**

## Exercise 6 — Responsive Card Grid

Set:

```
.card {
  flex: 1 1 250px;
}
```

Resize the browser and observe:

- Cards wrapping
- Cards resizing

# 8. Aligning Wrapped Rows

When items wrap, you can align rows using:

```
aligncontent: spacebetween;
```

⚠ This only works when wrapping is enabled.

## Exercise 7 — Row Alignment

Test:

- flexstart
- center
- spacearound

Observe row spacing changes.

## 9. Common Flexbox Responsiveness Mistakes

### ❌ Fixed Widths Everywhere

Avoid:

```
width: 400px;
```

Prefer:

```
flex: 1 1 300px;
```

### ❌ Forgetting Wrapping

No wrap = broken mobile layouts.

### ❌ Overusing Media Queries Too Early

Flexbox often solves layout issues *without* breakpoints.

## 10. Learning Object — Think in Constraints

### Exercise 8 — ConstraintBased Thinking

Ask:

- What is the minimum space this item needs?
- What should happen when space runs out?

Then encode that logic using Flexbox.

## 11. MicroExperiments (Vibe Learning Core)

### Exercise 9 — Resize & Observe

Continuously resize the browser and:

- Predict behavior
- Observe outcomes
- Adjust rules

### Exercise 10 — Compare Two Layouts

Create:

- Fixedwidth version
- Flexbased version

Which adapts better?

# AI Prompts (Chapter 9)

## Prompt 1 — Responsive Debugging

```
"My layout breaks on small screens. Ask me questions to diagnose the
Flexbox issue."
```

## Prompt 2 — Flex Property Breakdown

```
"Explain what this flex value is doing in plain language."
```

## Prompt 3 — Layout Strategy

```
"How would you design this layout to be responsive using Flexbox?"
```

## Prompt 4 — Best Practices

```
"What Flexbox patterns are most common in modern web design?"
```

# Mini Project — Responsive Feature Grid

## Exercise 11

Build a responsive features section:

```
<div class="features">
  <div class="feature">Fast</div>
  <div class="feature">Responsive</div>
  <div class="feature">Accessible</div>
  <div class="feature">Modern</div>
</div>
.features {
  display: flex;
  flexwrap: wrap;
  gap: 20px;
}
.feature {
  flex: 1 1 200px;
  padding: 20px;
  background: #fff;
  border: 1px solid #ddd;
}
```

Test at different widths.

# Knowledge Check (Quiz + Explanations)

## Q1: What does flexwrap: wrap do?

A) Shrinks items

B) Centers items

C) Allows items to move to new rows

D) Removes spacing

**Answer: C**

## Q2: What does flex: 1 1 250px mean?

A) Fixed width

B) Grow only

C) Flexible with a base size

D) No resizing

**Answer: C**

## Q3: Which property aligns wrapped rows?

A) `alignitems`

B) `justifycontent`

C) `aligncontent`

D) `flexgrow`

**Answer: C**

# Reflection (Vibe Learning)

Answer:

- What made your layout responsive today?
- What Flexbox concept finally "clicked"?
- Where do you still feel unsure?

## Chapter WrapUp

Today you:

Enabled wrapping

Controlled flexible sizing

Built responsive layouts

Learned to think in constraints

## Day 10 Preview

**Responsive Design Fundamentals: Media Queries & MobileFirst Thinking**

You'll learn when Flexbox isn't enough — and how to adapt layouts intentionally across screen sizes.

# 10

# Responsive Design Fundamentals: Mobile-First & Media Queries

**Day 10 of 30**

## Learning Objectives

By the end of this chapter, you will be able to:

- Explain what responsive design is and why it matters
- Understand the mobilefirst design philosophy
- Use media queries to adapt layouts across screen sizes
- Decide when a media query is needed (and when it isn't)
- Combine Flexbox and media queries effectively
- Avoid common responsive design mistakes
- Use AI prompts to reason about layout decisions across devices

## Vibe Learning Mindset (Chapter Focus)

"Design for constraints first — then enhance."

Responsive design isn't about guessing device sizes.

It's about designing for **limited space**, then expanding gracefully.

## What You're Building Today

You'll make your website **fully responsive** by:

- Designing for small screens first
- Enhancing layouts for larger screens
- Using media queries to adapt structure, spacing, and alignment

By the end of today, your site will work comfortably on:

- Phones
- Tablets
- Desktops

## 1. What Is Responsive Design (Really)?

Responsive design means:

A website adapts its layout, spacing, and content presentation based on available screen space.

This includes:

- Width
- Orientation
- Device capabilities

Responsive design is **usercentered**, not devicecentered.

## 2. MobileFirst Thinking

### The Old Way (DesktopFirst)

- Design for large screens
- Try to "shrink" things later
- Results in cramped mobile layouts

### The Modern Way (MobileFirst)

- Design for small screens first
- Add complexity only when space allows

If it works on a phone, it will scale up.

## Exercise 1 — Mobile Perspective

Open your site on:

- A narrow browser window
- A phone (or emulator)

Ask:

- Is content readable?
- Is navigation usable?
- Is anything unnecessary?

# 3. Media Queries: Conditional CSS

Media queries allow CSS to apply **only under certain conditions.**

Basic syntax:

```
@media (minwidth: 768px) {
  /* styles apply at 768px and up */
}
```

This means:

"Only apply these styles when the screen is at least 768px wide."

# 4. Common Breakpoints (Guidelines, Not Rules)

Typical reference points:

a. 480px — small phones
b. 480px — small phones
c. 768px — tablets
d. 1024px+ — desktops

⚠ These are **guidelines**, not requirements.

## Vibe Rule:

Don't design for devices. Design for layout needs.

## 5. MobileFirst CSS Structure

Start with **base styles** (mobile):

```
body {
  fontfamily: Arial, sansserif;
}
.nav {
  display: flex;
  flexdirection: column;
}
```

Enhance for larger screens:

```
@media (minwidth: 768px) {
  .nav {
    flexdirection: row;
    justifycontent: spacebetween;
  }
}
```

### Exercise 2 — MobileFirst Nav

- Stack nav links vertically by default
- Switch to horizontal layout on larger screens

Resize and observe behavior.

## 6. Adapting Layouts with Media Queries

Media queries can adjust:

- Layout direction
- Spacing
- Font sizes
- Visibility

### Example — Layout Enhancement

```
.cards {
  display: flex;
  flexdirection: column;
```

```
  gap: 16px;
}
@media (minwidth: 900px) {
  .cards {
    flexdirection: row;
  }
}
```

### Exercise 3 — Layout Shift

Apply:

- Column layout for small screens
- Row layout for large screens

Observe improved usability.

## 7. Typography & Spacing Responsiveness

Text must adapt too.

### Example — Responsive Font Size

```
body {
  fontsize: 16px;
}
@media (minwidth: 1024px) {
  body {
    fontsize: 18px;
  }
}
```

### Exercise 4 — Readability Test

Adjust:

- Font sizes
- Line spacing
- Section padding

Test readability at different widths.

## 8. Showing & Hiding Content Responsively

Sometimes content should:

- Appear on large screens
- Be hidden on small screens

### Example

```
.desktoponly {
  display: none;
}
@media (minwidth: 768px) {
  .desktoponly {
    display: block;
  }
}
```

### Exercise 5 — Conditional Content

Add:

- Mobileonly message
- Desktoponly enhancement

Use responsibly.

## 9. Common Responsive Design Mistakes

### ❌ Too Many Breakpoints

More breakpoints ≠ better design.

### ❌ Relying Only on Media Queries

Flexbox often solves problems without breakpoints.

### ❌ Hiding Core Content

Never hide essential information on mobile.

## 10. Learning Object — Breakpoint Reasoning

### Exercise 6 — Ask "Why"

For each media query, answer:

- What problem does this solve?
- What changes without it?

If you can't answer — you don't need it.

## 11. MicroExperiments (Vibe Learning Core)

### Exercise 7 — Resize & Predict

Resize your browser and:

- Predict what should happen
- Observe what actually happens

Adjust accordingly.

### Exercise 8 — Simplify

Remove one media query.

Does the layout still work?

## AI Prompts (Chapter 10)

### Prompt 1 — Responsive Review

```
"Review my responsive CSS and suggest improvements for mobile usability."
```

### Prompt 2 — Breakpoint Strategy

```
"Based on this layout, where would breakpoints be useful and why?"
```

### Prompt 3 — MobileFirst Coaching

```
"How can I simplify this layout for small screens?"
```

### Prompt 4 — Accessibility Check

```
"Does my responsive design negatively affect accessibility?"
```

# Mini Project — Responsive Page Upgrade

## Exercise 9

Enhance your site so:

- Navigation adapts by screen size
- Cards wrap or stack appropriately
- Spacing increases on larger screens

Document your reasoning in comments.

# Knowledge Check (Quiz + Explanations)

## Q1: What does "mobilefirst" mean?

A) Design only for phones

B) Design for large screens first

C) Start with small screens, then enhance

D) Ignore desktops

**Answer: C**

## Q2: What does minwidth mean in a media query?

A) Apply below this width

B) Apply above this width

C) Apply only on phones

D) Disable CSS

**Answer: B**

## Q3: When should you use a media query?

A) Always

B) Only when Flexbox fails

C) When layout needs to adapt

D) Never

**Answer: C**

## Reflection (Vibe Learning)

Answer:

- How did mobilefirst thinking change your design?
- What breakpoint felt truly necessary?
- What felt unnecessary?

## Chapter WrapUp

Today you:

Learned responsive design fundamentals

Applied mobilefirst thinking

Used media queries intentionally

Built adaptable layouts

## Day 11 Preview

### CSS Grid Fundamentals: TwoDimensional Layouts

You'll learn when Flexbox isn't enough — and how Grid gives you full layout control.

# 11

# CSS Grid Fundamentals: Two-Dimensional Layouts

**Day 11 of 30**

## Learning Objectives

By the end of this chapter, you will be able to:

- Explain when and why CSS Grid is the right layout tool
- Understand the difference between Grid and Flexbox
- Create grid containers and grid items
- Define rows and columns using gridtemplatecolumns and gridtemplaterows
- Use gaps to control spacing cleanly
- Place items intentionally within a grid
- Combine Grid with responsive design principles
- Use AI prompts to reason about layout structure instead of guessing

## Vibe Learning Mindset (Chapter Focus)

"Layout is a system, not a collection of hacks."

Flexbox works in **one direction**. Grid works in **two directions — rows and columns at the same time.**

Grid lets you design **entire page structures** intentionally.

## What You're Building Today

You'll refactor part of your website layout using **CSS Grid**, including:

- Multicolumn sections
- Structured content areas
- Responsive grids that adapt naturally

By the end of today, your layouts will feel **architected**, not improvised.

## 1. When to Use Grid vs Flexbox

### Use Flexbox When:

- You're laying items out in a single row or column
- Alignment and spacing are the main concern
- Content size should dictate layout

### Use Grid When:

- You control rows and columns
- The layout structure comes first
- You're building page sections or full layouts

Flexbox aligns content. Grid defines structure.

## 2. The Grid Mental Model

A Grid layout consists of:

a. A grid container
b. Grid tracks (rows & columns)
c. Grid cells
d. Grid items

```
.container {
  display: grid;
}
```

Once Grid is enabled, the browser thinks in **rows and columns.**

# 3. Defining Columns

## Basic Grid Columns

```
.container {
  display: grid;
  gridtemplatecolumns: 1fr 1fr 1fr;
}
```

This creates **three equal columns.**

## The fr Unit (Fractional Space)

`fr` means:

"Take a portion of available space."

Examples:

```
gridtemplatecolumns: 1fr 2fr;
```

The second column is twice as wide as the first.

## Exercise 1 — Column Control

Create grids with:

- 2 equal columns
- 3 unequal columns
- One fixed + one flexible column

# 4. Defining Rows

Rows work the same way.

```
gridtemplaterows: auto auto;
```

Rows typically adjust to content size.

## Exercise 2 — Row Awareness

Add:

- A header row
- A content row
- A footer row

Observe how content fills space.

## 5. Gaps: Clean Spacing Between Grid Items

Instead of margins:

```
.container {
  gap: 20px;
}
```

You can also define:

```
rowgap: 20px;
columngap: 10px;
```

### Exercise 3 — Spacing Consistency

Adjust gap values and observe:

- Visual balance
- Readability
- Layout clarity

## 6. Grid Items & Placement Basics

By default, items fill grid cells in order.

```
<div class="grid">
  <div>One</div>
  <div>Two</div>
  <div>Three</div>
</div>
```

### Manual Placement (Intro)

```
.item {
  gridcolumn: 1 / 3;
}
```

This spans **two columns.**

### Exercise 4 — Item Placement

Make one item:

- Span multiple columns
- Stand out visually

# 7. RealWorld Example: Content Grid

## HTML

```
<section class="features">
  <div class="feature">Fast</div>
  <div class="feature">Responsive</div>
  <div class="feature">Accessible</div>
  <div class="feature">Modern</div>
</section>
```

## CSS

```
.features {
  display: grid;
  gridtemplatecolumns: repeat(2, 1fr);
  gap: 20px;
}
```

## Exercise 5 — Grid Refactor

Convert a Flexbox layout into Grid.Which feels simpler?

# 8. Responsive Grid with autofit & minmax

This is where Grid shines.

```
.grid {
  display: grid;
  gridtemplatecolumns: repeat(autofit, minmax(200px, 1fr));
}
```

This means:

- Columns adjust automatically
- Layout adapts without media queries

## Exercise 6 — Resize & Observe

Resize the browser and watch columns:

- Expand
- Collapse
- Reflow naturally

## 9. Grid + Media Queries (Optional Enhancement)

Grid reduces the need for media queries — but they still help.

```
@media (minwidth: 900px) {
  .layout {
    gridtemplatecolumns: 250px 1fr;
  }
}
```

### Exercise 7 — Layout Enhancement

Add a sidebar layout only on larger screens.

## 10. Common Grid Mistakes (And Fixes)

### ❌ Using Grid for Simple Rows

Flexbox is simpler for singledirection layouts.

### ❌ OverSpecifying Rows

Let content define row height unless needed.

### ❌ Mixing Layout Logic

Decide:

Grid for structure

Flexbox for alignment

## 11. Learning Object — Layout Planning

### Exercise 8 — Sketch Before Code

Sketch a layout:

- Header
- Main content
- Sidebar
- Footer

Then translate it into Grid.

## 12. MicroExperiments (Vibe Learning Core)

### Exercise 9 — Predict the Grid

Before refreshing:

- Predict column count
- Predict item placement

Then test.

### Exercise 10 — Simplify

Remove unnecessary grid rules.

Does the layout still work?

## AI Prompts (Chapter 11)

### Prompt 1 — Grid Strategy

```
"Is CSS Grid the right tool for this layout? Explain why."
```

### Prompt 2 — Responsive Help

```
"How can I make this grid adapt without media queries?"
```

### Prompt 3 — Debugging Grid

```
"Why isn't my grid item spanning correctly?"
```

### Prompt 4 — Refactoring Advice

```
"Refactor this layout using Grid more effectively."
```

## Mini Project — Responsive Grid Section

### Exercise 11

Build a responsive section using Grid:

Feature cards

Gallery

Blog previews

Use:

```
repeat(autofit, minmax())
```

Explain your layout logic in comments.

# Knowledge Check (Quiz + Explanations)

## Q1: When should you use Grid instead of Flexbox?

A) For styling text

B) For onedirection layouts

C) For twodimensional layouts

D) For animations

**Answer: C**

## Q2: What does 1fr represent?

A) Fixed width

B) One pixel

C) A fraction of available space

D) Full width

**Answer: C**

## Q3: What does autofit do?

A) Fix column count

B) Automatically fit columns based on space

C) Disable responsiveness

D) Replace Flexbox

**Answer: B**

## Reflection (Vibe Learning)

Answer:

- When does Grid feel easier than Flexbox?
- What layout finally made sense today?
- Where might you combine Grid and Flexbox?

## Chapter WrapUp

Today you:

Learned CSS Grid fundamentals

Built twodimensional layouts

Created responsive structures

Gained architectural layout control

## Day 12 Preview

### Typography & Color in Web Design: Readability, Hierarchy & Mood

You'll shift from layout to **visual communication** — making your designs *feel* professional.

# 12

# Typography & Color in Web Design: Readability, Hierarchy & Mood

**Day 12 of 30**

## Learning Objectives

By the end of this chapter, you will be able to:

- Explain why typography and color are core to good web design
- Choose readable fonts for web projects
- Create visual hierarchy using font size, weight, and spacing
- Apply color intentionally to support usability and emotion
- Understand basic color contrast and accessibility rules
- Build a simple, consistent design system
- Use AI prompts to evaluate and refine visual design decisions

## Vibe Learning Mindset (Chapter Focus)

"Design is communication." Before users interact with your site, they **read and feel it.**

Typography and color determine whether users:

- Stay or leave
- Feel confident or confused
- Trust the content or ignore it

## What You're Building Today

You'll transform your site from "technically correct" to **visually intentional** by:

- Improving text readability
- Creating hierarchy with typography
- Applying a controlled color palette

By the end of today, your site will **feel designed**, not accidental.

## 1. Why Typography Matters on the Web

Typography is not decoration. It is **how information is delivered**.

Good typography:

- Reduces cognitive load
- Guides the reader's eye
- Makes content scannable

Poor typography:

- Exhausts users
- Hides important information
- Feels unprofessional

## 2. Web Fonts: What You Actually Need to Know

### Serif vs SansSerif (Quick Rule)

- Serif fonts → traditional, editorial, formal
- Sansserif fonts → modern, clean, digitalfriendly

For beginners: Sansserif fonts are usually safer for body text on the web.

### System Fonts (BeginnerFriendly)

```
body {
  fontfamily: Arial, Helvetica, sansserif;
}
```

Benefits:

- Fast loading
- Familiar
- Reliable across devices

### Exercise 1 — Font Swap

Try switching between:

- Arial
- Helvetica
- Georgia
- Times New Roman

Observe how tone changes.

## 3. Font Size & Readability

### Base Font Size

```
body {
  fontsize: 16px;
}
```

16px is the web's **comfortable default.**

### Line Height (Critical!)

```
p {
  lineheight: 1.6;
}
```

Good line height:

- Improves readability
- Prevents eye strain

### Exercise 2 — Readability Test

Adjust:

- Font size
- Line height

Read a paragraph out loud. Does it feel comfortable?

# 4. Creating Visual Hierarchy with Typography

Hierarchy helps users understand:

- What is most important
- What comes next
- What is supporting detail

## Example Hierarchy

```
h1 {
  fontsize: 32px;
}
h2 {
  fontsize: 24px;
}
p {
  fontsize: 16px;
}
```

## Weight & Spacing Matter Too

```
h2 {
  fontweight: 600;
  marginbottom: 12px;
}
```

## Exercise 3 — Hierarchy Audit

Check your page:

- Can users scan it?
- Do headings stand out clearly?

Improve where needed.

# 5. Color Basics (Without Overwhelm)

Color communicates:

- Emotion
- Priority
- Interaction

But too much color causes confusion.

## Beginner Rule:

Use **fewer colors**, more intentionally.

## 6. Choosing a Simple Color Palette

Start with:

- 1 background color
- 1 primary text color
- 1 accent color

Example:

```
:root {
  bg: #f5f5f5;
  text: #333333;
  accent: #2c7be5;
}
```

## Use Variables (Optional but Powerful)

```
body {
  backgroundcolor: var(bg);
  color: var(text);
}
```

## Exercise 4 — Palette Creation

Create your own 3color palette. Apply it consistently.

## 7. Color Contrast & Accessibility

Low contrast makes text unreadable.

## Good Contrast Example

Dark text on light background

Light text on dark background

## Exercise 5 — Contrast Check

Test:

- Paragraph text
- Links
- Headings

Ask:

Can I read this comfortably?

# 8. Using Color for Meaning

Color should signal purpose:

- Links
- Buttons
- Highlights
- Alerts

## Example — Links

```
a {
  color: var(accent);
}
```

## Avoid:

- Coloring everything
- Using color alone to convey meaning

## Exercise 6 — Purposeful Color

Identify:

- What deserves emphasis?
- What should remain neutral?

Adjust accordingly.

## 9. Common Typography & Color Mistakes

### ❌ Too Many Fonts

Limit to:

- 1 font for body
- 1 font for headings (optional)

### ❌ Low Contrast

Pretty ≠ readable.

### ❌ Inconsistent Styling

Random font sizes and colors confuse users.

## 10. Learning Object — Design System Thinking

### Exercise 7 — Define Your Design Rules

Write down:

- Body font
- Heading sizes
- Color palette
- Spacing rules

Use these consistently.

## 11. MicroExperiments (Vibe Learning Core)

### Exercise 8 — Remove Color

Temporarily remove all colors. Is hierarchy still clear?

### Exercise 9 — One Change Rule

Change one typographic value at a time. Observe impact.

## AI Prompts (Chapter 12)

### Prompt 1 — Typography Review

```
"Review my typography choices for readability and hierarchy."
```

### Prompt 2 — Color Palette Help

```
"Suggest a simple, accessible color palette for a beginner website."
```

### Prompt 3 — UX Perspective

```
"How do typography and color affect user trust on this page?"
```

### Prompt 4 — Accessibility Check

```
"Does my color contrast meet accessibility guidelines?"
```

## Mini Project — Visual Polish Pass

### Exercise 10

Refine your site so:

- Text is easy to scan
- Headings guide attention
- Colors feel intentional
- Nothing feels accidental

Add comments explaining design choices.

## Knowledge Check (Quiz + Explanations)

### Q1: What is typography primarily about?

A) Decoration

B) Font trends

C) Communication and readability

D) CSS complexity

**Answer: C**

### Q2: What is a good base font size for body text?

A) 12px

B) 14px

C) 16px

D) 24px

**Answer: C**

## Q3: Why limit color usage?

A) Browsers limit colors

B) Fewer colors improve clarity

C) It loads faster

D) It avoids CSS

**Answer: B**

## Reflection (Vibe Learning)

Answer:

a. How did typography change how your site feels?
b. What color decision felt hardest?
c. What design rule will you follow going forward?

## Chapter WrapUp

Today you:

Improved readability

Created visual hierarchy

Applied color intentionally

Made your design feel professional

## Day 13 Preview

### Buttons, Forms & User Interaction Design

You'll learn how users interact with your site — and how design guides action.

# 13

# Buttons, Forms & User Interaction Design

**Day 13 of 30**

## Learning Objectives

By the end of this chapter, you will be able to:

- Explain the role of buttons and forms in user interaction
- Create accessible buttons using HTML and CSS
- Design clear, usable forms
- Style inputs, labels, and buttons consistently
- Understand basic usability and accessibility rules for forms
- Guide user actions through visual design
- Use AI prompts to evaluate and improve interaction design

## Vibe Learning Mindset (Chapter Focus)

"Design tells users what to do — before text ever does."

Buttons and forms are **decision points**. Good interaction design:

- Reduces hesitation
- Builds confidence
- Prevents mistakes

Poor interaction design causes frustration — even if the code works.

## What You're Building Today

You'll add real interaction elements to your website, including:

- Calltoaction buttons
- A simple contact form
- Clearly styled input fields
- Visual cues that guide user behavior

By the end of today, your site will feel **interactive and intentional.**

## 1. Buttons vs Links (Critical Distinction)

### Use a Link When:

- Navigating to another page
- Opening external content

```
<a href="/about.html">About</a>
```

### Use a Button When:

- Triggering an action
- Submitting a form
- Performing an interaction

```
<button>Submit</button>
```

This distinction matters for accessibility and meaning.

## 2. Creating Buttons with HTML

### Basic Button

```
<button>Click Me</button>
```

### Button Inside a Form

```
<form>
  <button type="submit">Send</button>
</form>
```

Common types:

- submit
- reset
- button

## Exercise 1 — Button Audit

Review your site:

- Where should buttons exist?
- Where should links remain links?

# 3. Styling Buttons with CSS

Buttons should:

- Look clickable
- Stand out from text
- Feel consistent

## Basic Button Style

```
button {
  padding: 12px 20px;
  fontsize: 16px;
  backgroundcolor: var(accent);
  color: white;
  border: none;
  borderradius: 4px;
  cursor: pointer;
}
```

## Hover State (Feedback!)

```
button:hover {
  backgroundcolor: #1f5fc4;
}
```

### Exercise 2 — Button Variations

Create:

- Primary button
- Secondary button
- Disabledlooking button

## 4. Forms: How Users Give You Information

Forms allow users to:

a. Contact you
b. Sign up
c. Log in
d. Search

Good forms feel simple and respectful.

## 5. Basic Form Structure

```
<form>
  <label for="name">Name</label>
  <input type="text" id="name" />
  <label for="email">Email</label>
  <input type="email" id="email" />
  <button type="submit">Send</button>
</form>
```

### Why Labels Matter

Labels:

- Improve accessibility
- Increase usability
- Make inputs easier to click

Never rely on placeholder text alone.

## 6. Common Input Types

```
<input type="text" />
<input type="email" />
<input type="password" />
<textarea></textarea>
```

Choose input types carefully — browsers help users automatically.

### Exercise 3 — Input Selection

Add:

- Text input
- Email input
- Message textarea

Observe how browsers behave differently.

## 7. Styling Forms for Clarity

Forms should be:

- Easy to scan
- Easy to complete
- Visually grouped

### Basic Form Styles

```
form {
  maxwidth: 400px;
}
label {
  display: block;
  margintop: 16px;
}
input, textarea {
  width: 100%;
  padding: 10px;
  margintop: 4px;
}
```

### Exercise 4 — Form Readability

Improve:

- Spacing
- Alignment
- Visual grouping

## 8. Accessibility Basics for Forms

Accessibility is not optional.

### Key Rules:

- Every input has a label
- Buttons are keyboardaccessible
- Contrast is sufficient

### Exercise 5 — Accessibility Check

Try:

- Navigating your form using only the keyboard
- Clicking labels to focus inputs

## 9. Visual Cues & User Confidence

Users need feedback.

Examples:

- Hover effects
- Focus states
- Clear calltoaction text

### Example — Focus State

```
input:focus {
  outline: 2px solid var(accent);
}
```

## Exercise 6 — Feedback Design

Add focus styles to:

- Inputs
- Buttons

Test usability.

# 10. Common Interaction Design Mistakes

## ❌ Unclear Button Labels

Avoid:

- "Submit"
- "Click Here"

Prefer:

- "Send Message"
- "Sign Up"
- "Save Changes"

## ❌ Too Many Actions

One page → one primary action.

## ❌ Poor Spacing

Crowded forms increase errors.

# 11. Learning Object — Interaction Flow

## Exercise 7 — User Journey

Ask:

- What is the main action?
- Is it obvious?
- What happens after the action?

Improve flow accordingly.

# 12. MicroExperiments (Vibe Learning Core)

## Exercise 8 — Button Language

Change button text only. Observe how meaning changes.

## Exercise 9 — Simplify

Remove one input. Does the form feel easier?

# AI Prompts (Chapter 13)

## Prompt 1 — UX Review

```
"Review my buttons and form design from a usability perspective."
```

## Prompt 2 — Accessibility Help

```
"Are my form elements accessible? What can I improve?"
```

## Prompt 3 — Interaction Copy

```
"Suggest clearer button labels for this form."
```

## Prompt 4 — User Psychology

```
"How does button placement affect user behavior?"
```

# Mini Project — Contact Section

## Exercise 10

Add a polished contact section:

- Heading
- Short explanation
- Form with 2–3 inputs
- Clear calltoaction button

Comment on design decisions.

## Knowledge Check (Quiz + Explanations)

### Q1: When should you use a <button> instead of a link?

A) For navigation

B) For styling

C) For actions

D) Always

**Answer: C**

### Q2: Why are labels important?

A) Decoration

B) SEO only

C) Accessibility and usability

D) Styling

**Answer: C**

### Q3: What improves user confidence?

A) More fields

B) Clear feedback and spacing

C) Smaller text

D) Hidden actions

**Answer: B**

## Reflection (Vibe Learning)

Answer:

a. Which interaction felt most natural?
b. Where did users need more guidance?
c. What design rule will you apply to all future forms?

## Chapter WrapUp

Today you:

Designed usable buttons

Built accessible forms

Guided user interaction

Improved user confidence

## Day 14 Preview

### JavaScript Foundations: Bringing Websites to Life

You'll finally introduce JavaScript — carefully, clearly, and without fear.

# 14

# JavaScript Foundations: Bringing Websites to Life

**Day 14 of 30**

## Learning Objectives

By the end of this chapter, you will be able to:

- Explain what JavaScript is and what it does in the browser
- Understand how JavaScript connects to HTML
- Use the browser console confidently
- Create variables and understand basic data types
- Write simple JavaScript statements that produce visible results
- Read JavaScript code out loud and explain what it does
- Use AI prompts to reinforce understanding—not replace learning

## Vibe Learning Mindset (Chapter Focus)

You'll add **your first JavaScript behavior** to your website, including:

- Logging messages to the console
- Storing information in variables
- Connecting JavaScript to your HTML page

By the end of today, your site will **react**, not just display.

# 1. What Is JavaScript (In Plain Terms)?

JavaScript is the language that allows websites to:

- Respond to user actions
- Make decisions
- Change content dynamically
- React without reloading the page

If:

- HTML is structure
- CSS is appearance

Then:

JavaScript is **behavior and logic**

## What JavaScript Is NOT

- It is not Java
- It is not only for advanced developers
- It is not magic

JavaScript runs **inside the browser** and follows clear rules.

# 2. How JavaScript Fits into a Web Page

JavaScript can be added to a page in two ways:

- Inline (inside HTML)
- External file (best practice)

## External JavaScript File (Recommended)

Create a file: script.js

Link it in your HTML **before the closing** </body> **tag:**

```
<script src="script.js"></script>
```

Why here?

- HTML loads first
- JavaScript runs after elements exist

## Exercise 1 — Script Connection Test

Add this to `script.js`:

```
console.log("JavaScript is connected!");
```

Open your page → Rightclick → Inspect → Console

If you see the message, JavaScript is working.

# 3. The Browser Console (Your Best Friend)

The console is where JavaScript:

- Talks to you
- Reports errors
- Shows values

## Using console.log()

```
console.log("Hello from JavaScript");
```

This does **not** show on the page. It shows in the console.

```
The console is a safe playground.
```

## Exercise 2 — Console Experiments

Try logging:

- Your name
- A number
- A sentence

Change values and refresh.

# 4. Variables: Storing Information

Variables allow JavaScript to **remember things.**

## Creating Variables

```
let message = "Hello World";
```

Read this as:

"Create a variable called `message` and store the text 'Hello World'."

### Logging Variables

```
console.log(message);
```

### Exercise 3 — Variable Practice

Create variables for:

- Your name
- Your learning goal
- The current day number

Log each one.

## 5. Data Types (Just the Essentials)

JavaScript works with different types of data.

### Strings (Text)

```
let name = "Alex";
```

### Numbers

```
let day = 14;
```

### Booleans (True / False)

```
let isLearning = true;
```

### Exercise 4 — Identify the Type

Create one variable of each type. Log them and describe what they represent.

## 6. Reading JavaScript Like a Human

Don't rush. Read code out loud.

```
let count = 3;
count = count + 1;
console.log(count);
```

Read as:

- Start with count = 3
- Add 1 to count
- Log the result

Result: 4

### Exercise 5 — Predict First

Before refreshing the page:

- Predict the console output
- Then test

Prediction builds intuition.

## 7. Changing the Web Page (First Taste)

JavaScript can interact with HTML.

### Selecting an Element

```
document.querySelector("h1");
```

This finds the first `<h1>` on the page.

### Changing Text

```
document.querySelector("h1").textContent = "JavaScript Changed This!";
```

Refresh and observe.

### Exercise 6 — Page Interaction

Change:

- A heading's text
- A paragraph's text

See cause → effect.

## 8. Common Beginner JavaScript Mistakes

### ❌ Forgetting to Refresh

JavaScript changes run on page load.

### ❌ Typos

JavaScript is casesensitive.

### ❌ Panic on Errors

Errors are feedback, not failure.

Read them carefully.

## 9. Learning Object — Cause & Effect Thinking

### Exercise 7 — Trace the Logic

Write 3 lines of JavaScript.

Explain:

- What happens first
- What happens next
- What changes

## 10. MicroExperiments (Vibe Learning Core)

### Exercise 8 — One Line at a Time

Comment out one line:

```
// console.log(message);
```

Observe what changes.

### Exercise 9 — Change Values

Change variable values.

Observe different outcomes.

## AI Prompts (Chapter 14)

### Prompt 1 — Code Explanation

```
"Explain this JavaScript code line by line in plain language."
```

### Prompt 2 — Beginner Debugging

```
"I'm getting a JavaScript error. Ask me questions to help me understand
it."
```

## Prompt 3 — Concept Reinforcement

```
"Explain JavaScript variables using realworld examples."
```

## Prompt 4 — Learning Strategy

```
"What should I focus on first when learning JavaScript as a beginner?"
```

# Mini Project — JavaScript Introduction Demo

## Exercise 10

Add JavaScript that:

- Logs a welcome message
- Stores your name in a variable
- Changes a heading text when the page loads

Comment each line explaining *why* it exists.

# Knowledge Check (Quiz + Explanations)

## Q1: What does JavaScript primarily do?

A) Styles content

B) Structures content

C) Adds behavior and logic

D) Hosts websites

Answer: C

## Q2: Where should external JavaScript usually be linked?

A) Inside `<head>`

B) Inside `<footer>`

C) Before `</body>`

D) Anywhere

Answer: C

## Q3: What is a variable?

A) A function

B) A stored value

C) A style

D) An element

Answer: B

## Reflection (Vibe Learning)

Answer:

a. What surprised you about JavaScript?
b. What felt easier than expected?
c. What still feels confusing?

## Chapter WrapUp

Today you:

Connected JavaScript to a webpage

Used the browser console

Created variables

Changed page content dynamically

## Day 15 Preview

JavaScript Events: Responding to User Actions

You'll make your website react to clicks, input, and interaction.

# 15

# JavaScript Events: Responding to User Actions

**Day 15 of 30**

## Learning Objectives

By the end of this chapter, you will be able to:

- Explain what JavaScript events are in plain language
- Connect user actions (clicks, typing) to JavaScript logic
- Add event listeners to elements safely
- Write basic event handler functions
- Understand the flow: user action → event → response
- Understand the flow: user action → event → response
- Avoid common beginner mistakes with events
- Use AI prompts to debug and reason about interactions

## Vibe Learning Mindset (Chapter Focus)

"Events turn static pages into experiences."

JavaScript events are not complicated — they are **signals**:

"Something just happened."

Your job is to decide:

- What happened?
- What should we do about it?

## What You're Building Today

You'll make your website **react to user actions**, including:

- Clicking a button
- Triggering a response
- Changing content dynamically

By the end of today, your site will **listen and respond.**

## 1. What Is an Event?

An **event** is something that happens in the browser:

- A user clicks
- A key is pressed
- A form is submitted
- A page loads

JavaScript can **listen** for these events and respond.

### RealWorld Analogy

- Doorbell rings → You answer the door
- Button clicked → JavaScript runs code

## 2. The Event Flow (Big Picture)

Every event follows this pattern:

- User performs an action
- Browser detects the event
- JavaScript responds with code

Events connect **people** to **logic**.

## 3. Selecting Elements for Events

Before reacting, JavaScript must **find the element**.

```
const button = document.querySelector("button");
```

This selects the first `<button>` on the page.

### Exercise 1 — Element Selection

Select:

- A button
- A heading
- A paragraph

Log them to the console.

## 4. Adding an Event Listener

The modern way to handle events:

```
button.addEventListener("click", function () {
  console.log("Button was clicked!");
});
```

Read this as:

"When the button is clicked, run this code."

### Why addEventListener?

- Clean
- Flexible
- Multiple listeners allowed

Avoid older inline event styles.

## 5. Your First Interactive Button

### HTML

```
<button id="changeText">Click Me</button>
<p id="message">Nothing has happened yet.</p>
```

## JavaScript

```
const button = document.querySelector("#changeText");
const message = document.querySelector("#message");
button.addEventListener("click", function () {
  message.textContent = "The button was clicked!";
});
```

Click the button and observe the change.

### Exercise 2 — Modify the Response

Change:

- The message text
- The button label
- The element being updated

## 6. Understanding Event Handlers

The function inside `addEventListener` is called an **event handler**.

```
function handleClick() {
  console.log("Clicked!");
}
button.addEventListener("click", handleClick);
```

This keeps code cleaner and reusable.

### Exercise 3 — Named Function

Rewrite your click logic using a named function.

## 7. Common Event Types (Beginner Essentials)

| Event | When it happens |
|---|---|
| `click` | User clicks |
| `input` | User types |
| `submit` | Form submitted |
| `mouseover` | Mouse enters |
| `mouseout` | Mouse leaves |

### Exercise 4 — Explore Events

Add a `mouseover` event to a paragraph.Change text when hovered.

## 8. Events and Forms (Intro)

Forms fire a `submit` event.

```
form.addEventListener("submit", function (event) {
  event.preventDefault();
  console.log("Form submitted!");
});
```

`event.preventDefault()` stops the page from reloading.

### Exercise 5 — Safe Form Handling

Add a submit listener to your form and log a message.

## 9. The event Object (First Look)

Every event gives you information.

```
button.addEventListener("click", function (event) {
  console.log(event);
});
```

This object tells you:

- What happened
- Where it happened
- What element triggered it

### Exercise 6 — Event Curiosity

Log the event object. Explore its properties.

## 10. Common Beginner Event Mistakes

### ❌ Forgetting to Select the Element

JavaScript can't listen to what it can't find.

### ❌ Misspelling Event Names

`"click"` ✔ `"Click"` ❌

## ❌ Inline Events

Avoid:

```
<button onclick="doSomething()">Click</button>
```

Use `addEventListener` instead.

# 11. Learning Object — Cause & Effect Mapping

## Exercise 7 — Event Mapping

Write:

- User action
- Event name
- JavaScript response

Example:

Click → `click` → Change text

# 12. MicroExperiments (Vibe Learning Core)

## Exercise 8 — Predict Before Click

Before clicking:

- Predict what will happen
- Then test

## Exercise 9 — Remove the Listener

Comment out the event listener. Observe the difference.

# AI Prompts (Chapter 15)

## Prompt 1 — Event Explanation

```
"Explain JavaScript events like I've never coded before."
```

## Prompt 2 — Debugging Help

```
"My click event isn't working. Ask me diagnostic questions."
```

## Prompt 3 — Event Ideas

```
"Suggest beginnerfriendly interactive features using events."
```

## Prompt 4 — Code Review

```
"Review my eventhandling code for clarity and best practices."
```

## Mini Project — Interactive CalltoAction

### Exercise 10

Create:

a. A button

b. A message area

c. A click event that:

d. Changes text

e. Changes style

f. Logs to console

Comment each line explaining the logic.

## Knowledge Check (Quiz + Explanations)

### Q1: What is a JavaScript event?

A) A CSS animation

B) A user or browser action

C) A variable

D) A function

**Answer: B**

### Q2: What does addEventListener do?

A) Styles elements

B) Creates HTML

C) Listens for events

D) Reloads the page

**Answer: C**

## Q3: Why use event.preventDefault()?

A) Stop JavaScript

B) Stop default browser behavior

C) Create events

D) Add styling

**Answer: B**

## Reflection (Vibe Learning)

Answer:

a. What interaction felt most satisfying today?
b. What confused you at first?
c. How does this change how you think about websites?

## Chapter WrapUp

Today you:

Learned how events work

Responded to user actions

Built interactive features

Connected logic to behavior

## Day 16 Preview

**JavaScript Logic: Conditions, Decisions & User Feedback**

You'll teach your website how to **think and decide**.

# 16

# JavaScript Logic: Conditions, Decisions & User Feedback

**Day 16 of 30**

## Learning Objectives

By the end of this chapter, you will be able to:

- Explain what programmatic "logic" means in JavaScript
- Use conditional statements (if, else) to make decisions
- Compare values using comparison operators
- Combine conditions using logical operators
- Provide meaningful feedback to users based on conditions
- Predict how JavaScript will behave before running code
- Use AI prompts to reason through logic instead of guessing

## Vibe Learning Mindset (Chapter Focus)

"Logic is just asking questions — and responding honestly."

JavaScript logic is not about math. It's about **decisions**:

- Is this true or false?
- What should happen next?

## What You're Building Today

You'll teach your website to **make decisions**, including:

- Responding differently based on input
- Showing different messages
- Handling simple validation logic

By the end of today, your site will feel **aware**, not just reactive.

## 1. What Is Logic in JavaScript?

Logic is the ability to:

- Evaluate conditions
- Make choices
- Follow different paths

In real life:

- If it's raining → bring an umbrella
- If it's cold → wear a jacket

JavaScript works the same way.

## 2. Boolean Values: True or False

At the core of logic are **booleans**.

```
let isLoggedIn = true;
let isAdmin = false;
```

These values answer yes/no questions.

## Exercise 1 — Boolean Thinking

Create variables for:

- isLearning
- hasAccount
- isOver18

Log them to the console.

# 3. Comparison Operators

Comparison operators compare values.

| Operator | Meaning |
|---|---|
| === | Equal |
| !== | Not equal |
| > | Greater than |
| < | Less than |
| >= | Greater or equal |
| <= | Less or equal |

## Example

```
let age = 20;
console.log(age >= 18); // true
```

## Exercise 2 — Compare Values

Compare:

- Two numbers
- Two strings
- A number against a variable

Predict results before logging.

# 4. The if Statement (Core Decision Tool)

The basic structure:

```
if (condition) {
  // code runs if condition is true
}
```

## Example

```
let score = 80;
if (score >= 70) {
  console.log("You passed!");
}
```

### Exercise 3 — Simple Condition

Create an `if` statement that:

Checks a value

Logs a message if true

## 5. else: Handling the Other Path

```
if (score >= 70) {
  console.log("You passed!");
} else {
  console.log("Try again.");
}
```

Only **one path** runs.

### Exercise 4 — Two Outcomes

Create logic that:

- Shows one message if true
- Shows a different message if false

## 6. Multiple Conditions with else if

```
if (score >= 90) {
  console.log("Excellent");
} else if (score >= 70) {
  console.log("Good job");
} else {
  console.log("Needs improvement");
}
```

### Exercise 5 — Tiered Feedback

Create three outcome levels for:

- Score
- Age
- Input length

# 7. Logical Operators (&&, ||, !)

## AND (&&)

```
if (age >= 18 && hasAccount) {
  console.log("Access granted");
}
```

Both must be true.

## OR (||)

```
if (isAdmin || isModerator) {
  console.log("Special access");
}
```

Only one must be true.

## NOT (!)

```
if (!isLoggedIn) {
  console.log("Please log in");
}
```

### Exercise 6 — Combine Conditions

Write logic using:

a. &&

b. ||

c. !

Explain what each does.

# 8. Using Logic with User Interaction

## HTML

```
<input id="ageInput" type="number" />
<button id="checkAge">Check</button>
<p id="result"></p>
```

## JavaScript

```
const input = document.querySelector("#ageInput");
```

```
const button = document.querySelector("#checkAge");
const result = document.querySelector("#result");
button.addEventListener("click", function () {
  const age = Number(input.value);
  if (age >= 18) {
    result.textContent = "You are an adult.";
  } else {
    result.textContent = "You are under 18.";
  }
});
```

### Exercise 7 — Logic + Event

Modify the logic to:

- Add a third message
- Handle empty input

## 9. Guard Clauses (BeginnerFriendly Safety)

Stop bad input early.

```
if (!input.value) {
  result.textContent = "Please enter a value.";
  return;
}
```

This prevents deeper logic from running.

### Exercise 8 — Input Safety

Add a guard clause to your project.

## 10. Common Beginner Logic Mistakes

### ❌ Using = Instead of ===

Assignment ≠ comparison.

### ❌ Forgetting All Paths

Always consider:

- True case
- False case

## ❌ Overcomplicating Conditions

Simple logic is better logic.

# 11. Learning Object — Think in Questions

## Exercise 9 — Question Mapping

Write logic as questions:

- Is input empty?
- Is value greater than X?
- Is condition true?

Then convert to code.

# 12. MicroExperiments (Vibe Learning Core)

## Exercise 10 — Flip the Logic

Reverse a condition.

Predict the outcome.

Test it.

## Exercise 11 — Break It Safely

Introduce a logic error.

Read the result. Fix it.

# AI Prompts (Chapter 16)

## Prompt 1 — Logic Explanation

```
"Explain this conditional logic in plain English."
```

## Prompt 2 — Debugging Help

```
"My if/else logic isn't behaving as expected. Ask me questions."
```

## Prompt 3 — Practice Ideas

```
"Give me beginnerfriendly JavaScript logic exercises."
```

## Prompt 4 — Refactoring

```
"How can I simplify this conditional logic?"
```

# Mini Project — DecisionBased Interaction

## Exercise 12

Build a small feature that:

Takes user input

Uses at least two conditions

Shows different feedback messages

Explain your decision logic in comments.

# Knowledge Check (Quiz + Explanations)

## Q1: What do booleans represent?

A) Numbers

B) Strings

C) True/False values

D) Functions

Answer: C

## Q2: What does === check?

A) Assignment

B) Value only

C) Value and type

D) Existence

Answer: C

## Q3: Why use else if?

A) For styling

B) For multiple conditions

C) To stop JavaScript

D) For loops

Answer: B

## Reflection (Vibe Learning)

Answer:

What logic pattern felt most useful?

What decisionmaking felt hardest?

How does this change how you see websites?

## Chapter WrapUp

Today you:

Learned conditional logic

Made decisions in JavaScript

Combined events with logic

Gave meaningful user feedback

## Day 17 Preview

JavaScript Functions: Reusable Logic & Clean Code

You'll learn how to **organize and reuse** your JavaScript so it scales without chaos.

# 17

# JavaScript Functions: Reusable Logic & Clean Code

**Day 17 of 30**

## Learning Objectives

By the end of this chapter, you will be able to:

- Explain what a function is in plain language
- Create and call functions confidently
- Pass values into functions using parameters
- Return values from functions
- Refactor repeated code into reusable functions
- Read functions as intent, not syntax
- Use AI prompts to improve code clarity and structure

## Vibe Learning Mindset (Chapter Focus)

"If you copy code more than once, it wants to be a function."

Functions help you:

- Reduce repetition
- Improve clarity
- Think in actions instead of lines of code

This is where JavaScript starts to feel **organized instead of messy**.

## What You're Building Today

You'll refactor your JavaScript so that:

- Logic is grouped into meaningful functions
- Event handlers call reusable logic
- Your code reads like a story

By the end of today, your JavaScript will be **simpler, cleaner, and easier to change.**

## 1. What Is a Function?

A **function** is a reusable block of code that performs a task.

Think of it as:

- A recipe
- A set of instructions
- A named action

Instead of repeating steps, you **name them once.**

### RealWorld Analogy

Instead of explaining how to make coffee every time, you say: "Make coffee."

The details are already defined.

## 2. Creating Your First Function

Basic function structure:

```
function sayHello() {
  console.log("Hello!");
}
```

This **defines** the function.

### Calling the Function

```
sayHello();
```

Nothing happens until the function is **called.**

## Exercise 1 — Define & Call

Create a function that:

- Logs a welcome message
- Call it twice
- Observe how reuse works.

# 3. Functions with Parameters (Input)

Functions become powerful when they accept input.

```
function greet(name) {
  console.log("Hello " + name);
}
```

Call it like this:

```
greet("Alex");
greet("Jordan");
```

## How to Read This

"Create a function called `greet` that takes a `name` and uses it."

## Exercise 2 — Personalization

Create a function that:

- Accepts a user's name
- Displays a custom message

Change the input and observe different results.

# 4. Multiple Parameters

Functions can take more than one input.

```
function add(a, b) {
  console.log(a + b);
}
```

### Exercise 3 — MultiInput Function

Create a function that:

- Accepts two numbers
- Logs their sum

Predict the result before calling it.

## 5. Returning Values (Instead of Logging)

Logging shows information. **Returning** gives information back.

```
function add(a, b) {
  return a + b;
}
let result = add(3, 4);
console.log(result);
```

### Why return Matters

- Enables reuse
- Allows chaining logic
- Separates logic from display

### Exercise 4 — Return Practice

Create a function that:

- Returns a calculated value
- Use the returned value elsewhere

## 6. Functions + Events (Best Practice)

Instead of writing logic inside event listeners:

❌ Messy:

```
button.addEventListener("click", function () {
  // lots of logic here
});
```

Clean:

```
function handleClick() {
  console.log("Button clicked");
}
button.addEventListener("click", handleClick);
```

## Exercise 5 — Refactor Event Logic

Move event logic into a named function.

Notice how readability improves.

# 7. Refactoring Repeated Code

## Before (Repeated Logic)

```
console.log("Welcome!");
console.log('Today is Day 17');
```

## After (Function)

```
function showWelcome() {
  console.log("Welcome!");
  console.log("Today is Day 17");
}
```

## Exercise 6 — Spot the Pattern

Find any repeated code in your project. Turn it into a function.

# 8. Naming Functions Clearly

Good function names:

- Describe what they do
- Use verbs
- Are easy to read

Examples:

- showMessage
- checkAge
- updateHeading

Bad examples:

- doThing
- test
- x

### Exercise 7 — Rename for Clarity

Rename a function to better describe its purpose.

## 9. Scope (BeginnerFriendly Intro)

Variables created inside a function **stay inside.**

```
function test() {
  let message = "Inside";
}
console.log(message); // ❌ Error
```

This is **scope.**

### Why This Is Good

- Prevents conflicts
- Keeps code safe
- Encourages organization

### Exercise 8 — Scope Awareness

Create:

- One variable inside a function
- One outside
- Log both and observe behavior.

## 10. Common Beginner Function Mistakes

### ❌ Forgetting to Call the Function

Defining ≠ running.

### ❌ Too Many Responsibilities

One function → one job.

## ❌ Overusing Global Variables

Prefer passing values into functions.

# 11. Learning Object — Think in Actions

## Exercise 9 — Action Mapping

Write down:

- What actions your site performs
- Turn each into a function name

Example:

```
updateMessage
validateInput
showResult
```

# 12. MicroExperiments (Vibe Learning Core)

## Exercise 10 — Change the Function

Modify one function. Observe how all uses update automatically.

## Exercise 11 — Break & Fix

- Remove a `return`.
- See what breaks.
- Fix it.

# AI Prompts (Chapter 17)

## Prompt 1 — Function Explanation

```
"Explain what this function does line by line."
```

## Prompt 2 — Refactoring Help

```
"Refactor this JavaScript code using functions for clarity."
```

## Prompt 3 — Naming Advice

```
"Suggest better function names for this code."
```

## Prompt 4 — Learning Reinforcement

```
"Why are functions essential for clean JavaScript code?"
```

# Mini Project — FunctionDriven Feature

## Exercise 12

Build a feature that:

- Uses at least 3 functions
- One function handles logic
- One handles display
- One handles events
- Add comments explaining each role.

# Knowledge Check (Quiz + Explanations)

## Q1: What is a function?

A) A variable

B) A reusable block of code

C) An event

D) A loop

Answer: B

## Q2: What does return do?

A) Logs output

B) Stops JavaScript

C) Sends a value back

D) Creates a variable

Answer: C

## Q3: Why use functions?

A) To write more code

B) To organize and reuse logic

C) To style elements

D) To avoid JavaScript

Answer: B

## Reflection (Vibe Learning)

Answer:

a. How did functions change how you think about code?
b. What became easier today?
c. Where can you refactor more?

## Chapter WrapUp

Today you:

Learned what functions are

Reused logic cleanly

Improved readability

Built scalable JavaScript

## Day 18 Preview

JavaScript Arrays & Loops: Working with Lists of Data

You'll learn how websites handle **collections of information** efficiently.

# 18

# JavaScript Arrays & Loops: Working with Lists of Data

**Day 18 of 30**

## Learning Objectives

By the end of this chapter, you will be able to:

- Explain what arrays are and why they're essential in JavaScript
- Create and modify arrays confidently
- Access array values using indexes
- Use loops to process multiple items efficiently
- Combine arrays, loops, functions, and DOM updates
- Avoid common beginner mistakes with loops
- Use AI prompts to reason about iteration and data flow

## Vibe Learning Mindset (Chapter Focus)

"Real websites don't deal with one thing — they deal with collections."

Menus, posts, comments, products, messages — all of these are **lists**.

Arrays + loops are how JavaScript handles **scale**.

## What You're Building Today

You'll build features that:

- Store multiple values
- Display lists dynamically
- Process each item using logic

By the end of today, your site will handle **many things with one piece of code.**

## 1. What Is an Array?

An **array** is a list of values stored in a single variable.

```
let skills = ["HTML", "CSS", "JavaScript"];
```

Instead of:

```
let skill1 = "HTML";
let skill2 = "CSS";
let skill3 = "JavaScript";
```

You store them together.

### RealWorld Analogy

An array is like:

- A playlist
- A grocery list
- A todo list

Order matters.

## 2. Accessing Array Values (Indexing)

Arrays are **zeroindexed.**

```
skills[0]; // "HTML"
skills[1]; // "CSS"
skills[2]; // "JavaScript"
```

### Exercise 1 — Index Awareness

Log:

- The first item
- The last item

Hint:

```
skills.length  1
```

# 3. Updating Arrays

## Change an Item

```
skills[1] = "Advanced CSS";
```

## Add an Item

```
skills.push("React");
```

## Remove the Last Item

```
skills.pop();
```

## Exercise 2 — Modify the List

- Add two items
- Remove one
- Log the final array

# 4. Why Loops Exist

Loops allow you to:

- Repeat actions
- Process every item
- Avoid copypasting code

Without loops:

```
console.log(skills[0]);
console.log(skills[1]);
console.log(skills[2]);
```

With loops:

```
for (let i = 0; i < skills.length; i++) {
  console.log(skills[i]);
}
```

## 5. The for Loop (Beginner Core)

Basic structure:

```
for (let i = 0; i < skills.length; i++) {
  console.log(skills[i]);
}
```

Read it as:

- Start at index 0
- Keep going while i is less than the array length
- Increase i by 1 each time

### Exercise 3 — Loop Reading

Read the loop out loud. Explain what happens on each step.

## 6. Looping Through Arrays Safely

Use:

```
array.length
```

Never hardcode numbers: ❌ `i < 3`

`i < skills.length`

### Exercise 4 — Dynamic Safety

Change array size. Confirm the loop still works.

## 7. Displaying Arrays on the Page

### HTML

```
<ul id="skillList"></ul>
```

### JavaScript

```
const list = document.querySelector("#skillList");
skills.forEach(function (skill) {
  const li = document.createElement("li");
  li.textContent = skill;
  list.appendChild(li);
});
```

This creates list items dynamically.

### Exercise 5 — Dynamic Rendering

Change array values.

Refresh the page. Watch the list update automatically.

## 8. forEach: A Friendlier Loop

Instead of `for`:

```
skills.forEach(function (skill) {
  console.log(skill);
});
```

Benefits:

- Cleaner
- Fewer mistakes
- Easier to read

### Exercise 6 — Loop Swap

Rewrite a `for` loop using `forEach`.

## 9. Combining Loops with Logic

```
skills.forEach(function (skill) {
  if (skill === "JavaScript") {
    console.log("Core skill found!");
  }
});
```

Loops + conditions = power.

### Exercise 7 — Conditional Rendering

Highlight one item differently based on logic.

## 10. Common Beginner Loop Mistakes

### ❌ Infinite Loops

Forgetting to increment:

```
i++
```

### ❌ OffbyOne Errors

Using <= instead of <.

### ❌ Modifying the Array Incorrectly

Be careful when changing arrays inside loops.

## 11. Learning Object — Think in Collections

### Exercise 8 — Data Modeling

List:

- Navigation items
- Skills
- Features
- Tasks

Turn one into an array.

## 12. MicroExperiments (Vibe Learning Core)

### Exercise 9 — Predict the Output

Before running:

- Predict what logs
- Then test

### Exercise 10 — Change the Data

Change the array, not the code. Observe behavior.

## AI Prompts (Chapter 18)

### Prompt 1 — Array Explanation

```
"Explain JavaScript arrays using a realworld analogy."
```

### Prompt 2 — Loop Debugging

```
"My loop isn't working correctly. Ask me questions to diagnose it."
```

### Prompt 3 — Code Refactor

```
"Refactor this code to use arrays and loops instead of repetition."
```

## Prompt 4 — Practice Generator

```
"Give me beginnerfriendly array and loop exercises."
```

## Mini Project — Dynamic List Builder

### Exercise 11

Build a feature that:

- Stores items in an array
- Loops through them
- Displays them dynamically
- Uses logic to highlight one item

Explain your design choices in comments.

## Knowledge Check (Quiz + Explanations)

### Q1: What is an array?

A) A function

B) A loop

C) A list of values

D) A condition

Answer: C

### Q2: What index does an array start at?

A) 1

B) 1

C) 0

D) Depends

Answer: C

## Q3: Why use loops?

A) To slow down code

B) To repeat logic efficiently

C) To style elements

D) To create variables

Answer: B

## Reflection (Vibe Learning)

Answer:

a. What clicked about arrays today?
b. How do loops reduce effort?
c. Where might you use arrays in a real website?

## Chapter WrapUp

Today you:

Learned how arrays store data

Used loops to process lists

Displayed dynamic content

Scaled your JavaScript thinking

## Day 19 Preview

JavaScript Objects: Modeling RealWorld Data

You'll learn how to group related information — the way real applications do.

# 19

# JavaScript Objects: Modeling Real-World Data

**Day 19 of 30**

## Learning Objectives

By the end of this chapter, you will be able to:

- Explain what JavaScript objects are in plain language
- Create objects with properties and values
- Access and update object properties confidently
- Combine objects with arrays for realworld data modeling
- Loop through object data meaningfully
- Use objects to improve code clarity and structure
- Use AI prompts to reason about data modeling decisions

## Vibe Learning Mindset (Chapter Focus)

“Arrays store lists. Objects describe *things*.”

Real applications don’t just handle values — they handle **entities**: users, products, posts, settings.

Objects are how JavaScript understands the *real world.*

## What You're Building Today

You'll refactor your JavaScript so that:

- Related data lives together
- Code becomes more readable and meaningful
- Dynamic content becomes easier to manage

By the end of today, your code will feel **intentional**, not scattered.

## 1. What Is an Object?

An **object** groups related information together using **key–value pairs.**

```
let user = {
  name: "Alex",
  age: 25,
  isLearning: true
};
```

Instead of separate variables:

```
let name = "Alex";
let age = 25;
let isLearning = true;
```

You group them into **one concept**.

### RealWorld Analogy

An object is like:

- A contact card
- A profile
- A product description

Everything belongs together.

## 2. Object Properties & Values

Each property has:

- A key (name)
- A value

```
user.name; // "Alex"
user.age;  // 25
```

## Dot Notation (Most Common)

```
console.log(user.name);
```

## Bracket Notation (When Needed)

```
console.log(user["age"]);
```

Use brackets when:

- Property names come from variables
- Property names contain special characters

## Exercise 1 — Property Access

Log:

- One string value
- One number value
- One boolean value

# 3. Updating Object Properties

Objects are **mutable**.

```
user.age = 26;
user.isLearning = false;
```

## Adding New Properties

```
user.skill = "JavaScript";
```

## Exercise 2 — Update & Extend

- Update an existing value
- Add a new property
- Log the full object

# 4. Objects vs Arrays (Clarity Matters)

## Array Example

```
let skills = ["HTML", "CSS", "JavaScript"];
```

Use arrays for:

- Lists
- Ordered collections

## Object Example

```
let course = {
  title: "Modern Web Design",
  days: 30,
  level: "Beginner"
};
```

Use objects for:

- Describing things
- Grouping related info

Arrays hold *many items*. Objects describe *one item*.

# 5. Objects Inside Arrays (RealWorld Pattern)

Most real data looks like this:

```
let students = [
  { name: "Alex", level: "Beginner" },
  { name: "Jordan", level: "Intermediate" },
  { name: "Sam", level: "Beginner" }
];
```

## Exercise 3 — Loop Objects

Loop through the array and log:

- Each name
- Each level

# 6. Displaying Object Data on the Page

## HTML

```
<ul id="studentList"></ul>
```

## JavaScript

```
const list = document.querySelector("#studentList");
students.forEach(function (student) {
  const li = document.createElement("li");
  li.textContent = student.name + " – " + student.level;
  list.appendChild(li);
});
```

## Exercise 4 — Dynamic Display

Add a new student object

Refresh.

Observe automatic update.

# 7. Object Destructuring (BeginnerFriendly Intro)

Instead of:

```
let name = user.name;
let age = user.age;
```

You can write:

```
let { name, age } = user;
```

This improves readability.

## Exercise 5 — Destructure

Extract two properties using destructuring.

# 8. Looping Through Object Properties

## Using for...in

```
for (let key in user) {
  console.log(key + ": " + user[key]);
}
```

## Exercise 6 — Inspect an Object

Loop through your object and log all keys and values.

## 9. Why Objects Improve Code Quality

Without objects:

- Variables scatter
- Meaning gets lost
- Code becomes fragile

With objects:

- Intent is clear
- Changes are safer
- Code scales naturally

## 10. Common Beginner Object Mistakes

### ❌ Treating Objects Like Arrays

Objects don't have indexes.

### ❌ OverNesting Too Early

Keep structures simple.

### ❌ Inconsistent Property Names

Consistency improves clarity.

## 11. Learning Object — Data Modeling Thinking

### Exercise 7 — Model Something Real

Choose:

- A user profile
- A blog post
- A product

List its properties. Create an object.

## 12. MicroExperiments (Vibe Learning Core)

### Exercise 8 — Change One Property

Modify a value. Observe effect.

## Exercise 9 — Add One Property

Extend the object. Use it somewhere.

# AI Prompts (Chapter 19)

## Prompt 1 — Object Explanation

```
"Explain JavaScript objects using a realworld example."
```

## Prompt 2 — Data Modeling Help

```
"How should I structure this data using objects and arrays?"
```

## Prompt 3 — Refactoring Advice

```
"Refactor this code to use objects more effectively."
```

## Prompt 4 — Learning Reinforcement

```
"When should I use an object instead of multiple variables?"
```

# Mini Project — DataDriven Feature

## Exercise 10

Build a feature that:

- Uses an array of objects
- Loops through data
- Displays formatted information
- Uses logic to highlight one item

Explain your data structure in comments.

# Knowledge Check (Quiz + Explanations)

## Q1: What is an object?

A) A loop

B) A function

C) A group of related properties

D) A list

Answer: C

## Q2: When should you use an array?

A) To describe one thing

B) To store ordered lists

C) To group properties

D) To handle logic

Answer: B

## Q3: What does dot notation do?

A) Creates objects

B) Accesses object properties

C) Loops data

D) Deletes values

Answer: B

## Reflection (Vibe Learning)

Answer:

a. What felt clearer using objects?
b. How does this match realworld thinking?
c. Where would objects simplify your code?

## Chapter WrapUp

Today you:

Modeled realworld data

Used objects and arrays together

Improved code clarity

Prepared for larger applications

## Day 20 Preview

JavaScript DOM Manipulation: Creating & Updating Content Dynamically

You'll learn how JavaScript **builds and updates the page itself** — the core of modern frontend development.

# 20

# JavaScript DOM Manipulation: Creating & Updating Content Dynamically

**Day 20 of 30**

## Learning Objectives

By the end of this chapter, you will be able to:

- Explain what the DOM is and why it matters
- Select elements reliably using JavaScript
- Create new HTML elements dynamically
- Update, remove, and replace DOM content
- Combine DOM manipulation with arrays, objects, and events
- Understand performancefriendly DOM updates
- Use AI prompts to reason about DOM behavior and structure

## Vibe Learning Mindset (Chapter Focus)

"JavaScript doesn't just change pages — it *builds* them."

The DOM is how JavaScript **sees** your HTML. Once you understand this, frontend development becomes **logical instead of magical**.

## What You're Building Today

You'll build **dynamic page content** that:

- Is created entirely with JavaScript
- Updates based on data and logic
- Responds to user interaction

By the end of today, your page will feel **alive and datadriven.**

## 1. What Is the DOM?

DOM = **Document Object Model**

It is:

- A treelike representation of your HTML
- How the browser understands structure
- How JavaScript interacts with the page

Every HTML element becomes a **node** in the DOM.

### Mental Model

HTML:

```
<h1>Hello</h1>
<p>Welcome</p>
```

DOM:

```
document
 ├─ h1
 └─ p
```

JavaScript talks to this structure.

## 2. Selecting Elements (Quick Review)

JavaScript must **find elements** before changing them.

```
document.querySelector("h1");
document.querySelector("#main");
document.querySelector(".card");
```

## Best Practice

Use **specific selectors** to avoid surprises.

## Exercise 1 — Selection Confidence

Select:

- One element by tag
- One by ID
- One by class

Log them to the console.

# 3. Creating Elements Dynamically

This is where things level up.

```
const p = document.createElement("p");
p.textContent = "This was created by JavaScript";
```

At this point, the element exists **in memory only**.

## Adding It to the Page

```
document.body.appendChild(p);
```

Now it appears on the page.

## Exercise 2 — First Dynamic Element

Create:

- A paragraph
- A heading
- A list item

Append each to the page.

# 4. Building Content from Data

This is the heart of dynamic websites.

## Example Data

```
let topics = ["HTML", "CSS", "JavaScript"];
```

### Rendering with JavaScript

```
const ul = document.createElement("ul");
topics.forEach(function (topic) {
  const li = document.createElement("li");
  li.textContent = topic;
  ul.appendChild(li);
});
document.body.appendChild(ul);
```

### Exercise 3 — Data → DOM

Change the array.

Refresh the page. Observe how content updates automatically.

## 5. Updating Existing Elements

### Change Text

```
heading.textContent = "Updated Title";
```

### Change HTML (Use Carefully)

```
element.innerHTML = "<strong>Bold text</strong>";
```

Prefer `textContent` unless HTML is needed.

### Exercise 4 — Controlled Updates

Update:

- A heading
- A paragraph
- A list item

Use `textContent`.

## 6. Removing Elements

```
element.remove();
```

## Exercise 5 — Clean Up

Remove:

- One dynamically created element
- One existing element

Observe layout changes.

# 7. DOM Manipulation + Events

## Example

```
button.addEventListener("click", function () {
  const item = document.createElement("li");
  item.textContent = "New Item";
  list.appendChild(item);
});
```

Each click adds content.

## Exercise 6 — Click to Create

Create a button that:

- Adds items to a list
- Uses an array as the source

# 8. DOM Performance Basics (BeginnerSafe)

Avoid:

- Rebuilding the entire page repeatedly
- Excessive innerHTML

Prefer:

- Creating elements once
- Updating only what changes

# 9. Common Beginner DOM Mistakes

## ✗ Forgetting to Append

Creating elements without adding them does nothing.

### ❌ Overusing innerHTML

This can:

- Remove event listeners
- Remove event listeners
- Introduce bugs

### ❌ Mixing Data & DOM Logic

Keep:

- Data separate
- Rendering logic clear

## 10. Learning Object — DOM as a Bridge

### Exercise 7 — Map the Flow

Write out:

- Where data lives
- How it becomes DOM
- How users affect it

Understanding flow prevents bugs.

## 11. MicroExperiments (Vibe Learning Core)

### Exercise 8 — Predict First

Before clicking or refreshing:

- Predict what will change
- Then test

### Exercise 9 — Refactor

Move DOM creation into a function. Reuse it.

## AI Prompts (Chapter 20)

### Prompt 1 — DOM Explanation

```
"Explain the DOM using a realworld analogy."
```

## Prompt 2 — Debugging Help

```
"My DOM updates aren't showing. Ask me diagnostic questions."
```

## Prompt 3 — Code Review

```
"Review my DOM manipulation code for clarity and best practices."
```

## Prompt 4 — Architecture Thinking

```
"How should I separate data, logic, and DOM updates?"
```

## Mini Project — Dynamic Content Section

### Exercise 10

Build a feature that:

- Uses an array of objects
- Dynamically creates DOM elements
- Updates content on user interaction
- Removes items cleanly

Comment on your DOM strategy.

## Knowledge Check (Quiz + Explanations)

### Q1: What is the DOM?

A) A JavaScript library

B) A database

C) A structured representation of HTML

D) A CSS system

Answer: C

### Q2: What does createElement() do?

A) Finds elements

B) Deletes elements

C) Creates elements in memory

D) Styles elements

Answer: C

## Q3: Why prefer textContent?

A) Faster animations

B) Safer text updates

C) Better styling

D) Required for loops

Answer: B

# Reflection (Vibe Learning)

Answer:

a. How did dynamic DOM creation change how you think about websites?
b. What felt powerful today?
c. Where could this be useful in a real project?

# Chapter WrapUp

Today you:

Understood the DOM

Created elements dynamically

Updated and removed content

Built datadriven pages

# Day 21 Preview

Project 1: Building a Dynamic Personal Website (Part 1)

You'll start assembling everything you've learned into a **real, cohesive project**.

# 21

# Project 1: Building a Dynamic Personal Website (Part 1)

**Day 21 of 30**

## Learning Objectives

By the end of this chapter, you will be able to:

- Plan a complete beginnerfriendly website intentionally
- Translate ideas into HTML structure
- Apply layout, spacing, typography, and color systems
- Organize files cleanly for a real project
- Identify where JavaScript will add value (and where it shouldn't)
- Build the foundation of a dynamic personal website
- Use AI prompts as a design thinking partner, not a shortcut

## Vibe Learning Mindset (Chapter Focus)

"Projects aren't about showing everything you know —they're about solving one problem well.
"This project is **not** about perfection. It's about **clarity, structure, and intention**.

## What You're Building Today

You're building a **Dynamic Personal Website**, which includes:

- A clear introduction section

- A skills or interests section
- A content area that will become dynamic
- Clean layout and visual hierarchy

This project will evolve over the next few days.

# 1. Project Overview (What & Why)

## What Is This Website?

A simple personal website that:

- Introduces who you are
- Shows what you're learning or interested in
- Uses JavaScript to generate content dynamically

## Why This Project Matters

This project proves you can:

a. Design structure
b. Style intentionally
c. Add logic responsibly
d. Build something real

This is the bridge from "learning concepts" to **being a web developer**.

# 2. Project Planning (Before Writing Code)

## The Page Sections

Sketch or write down:

a. Header
b. Site title
c. Simple navigation (static for now)
d. Main Content
e. About section
f. Skills / Topics section (dynamic later)
g. Footer
h. Simple text or copyright

## Exercise 1 — Project Sketch

Draw or write:

- Section names
- Rough order
- What content goes where

No code yet.

# 3. File Structure (Professional Habit)

Create this structure:

```
project/
│
├─ index.html
├─ styles.css
└─ script.js
```

Why this matters:

- Separation of concerns
- Easier debugging
- Scales cleanly

## Exercise 2 — Setup

Create the files. Open `index.html` in your browser.

# 4. HTML Structure (Semantic First)

## Basic HTML Skeleton

```
<!DOCTYPE html>
<html lang="en">
<head>
  <meta charset="UTF8">
  <title>My Dynamic Website</title>
  <link rel="stylesheet" href="styles.css">
</head>
<body>
  <header>
```

```
    <h1>My Learning Journey</h1>
  </header>
  <main>
    <section id="about">
      <h2>About Me</h2>
      <p>I am learning modern web design.</p>
    </section>
    <section id="topics">
      <h2>What I'm Learning</h2>
      <! Dynamic content will go here >
    </section>
  </main>
  <footer>
    <p>© 2026</p>
  </footer>
  <script src="script.js"></script>
</body>
</html>
```

## Why This Structure Works

- Semantic tags improve readability
- Sections are easy to target
- JavaScript has clear insertion points

## Exercise 3 — Customize Content

Change:

- Site title
- About text
- Section headings

Make it *yours*.

# 5. Base Styling (Clarity Before Beauty)

## styles.css

```
* {
  boxsizing: borderbox;
}
```

```
body {
  margin: 0;
  fontfamily: Arial, Helvetica, sansserif;
  background: #f5f5f5;
  color: #333;
}
header, footer {
  background: #222;
  color: white;
  padding: 20px;
}
main {
  maxwidth: 900px;
  margin: auto;
  padding: 20px;
}
section {
  marginbottom: 40px;
}
```

### Exercise 4 — Layout Check

Open the page and check:

- Readability
- Spacing
- Alignment

Fix anything that feels uncomfortable.

## 6. Typography & Hierarchy (Apply What You Learned)

Add:

```
h1 {
  margin: 0;
}
h2 {
  marginbottom: 10px;
}
p {
```

```
  lineheight: 1.6;
}
```

### Exercise 5 — Hierarchy Audit

Ask:

- Is the main heading obvious?
- Are sections easy to scan?
- Is text comfortable to read?

Adjust as needed.

## 7. Planning the Dynamic Section (Before JavaScript)

### What Will Be Dynamic?

The "What I'm Learning" section will:

- Be generated from an array
- Update automatically if data changes
- Be created with JavaScript

### Data Preview (Don't Code Yet)

Example:

```
["HTML", "CSS", "JavaScript"]
```

Later, this becomes:

- A list
- Cards
- Interactive content

### Exercise 6 — Content Planning

Write down:

- 3–5 items you want to display dynamically
- What each item represents

## 8. Connecting JavaScript (Foundation Only)

### script.js

```
console.log("Project script connected");
```

Open the browser console to confirm.

### Exercise 7 — Connection Check

If the message appears: JavaScript is ready

If not:

- Check file name
- Check script placement

## 9. What We Are NOT Doing Yet (Important)

We are **not**:

- Adding complex logic
- Styling dynamic elements
- Handling user input

Why? Strong foundations prevent fragile projects.

## 10. Common Beginner Project Mistakes

### ❌ Starting with JavaScript First

Structure comes first.

### ❌ OverStyling Early

Clarity before polish.

### ❌ Skipping Planning

Planning saves hours later.

# 11. Learning Object — Project Thinking

## Exercise 8 — Explain Your Project

In one paragraph:

- What is this site?
- Who is it for?
- What does it demonstrate?

Clear explanation = clear thinking.

# 12. MicroExperiments (Vibe Learning Core)

## Exercise 9 — Change One Thing

Change one:

- Color
- Spacing
- Text

Observe how it affects the whole page.

## Exercise 10 — Break & Fix

Remove:

- A closing tag
- A CSS rule

Fix it intentionally.

# AI Prompts (Chapter 21)

## Prompt 1 — Project Review

```
"Review this beginner project structure and suggest improvements."
```

## Prompt 2 — Layout Advice

```
"Is my page layout clear and readable for a beginner audience?"
```

## Prompt 3 — Design Simplification

```
"What can I simplify in this design without losing clarity?"
```

## Prompt 4 — Learning Reflection

```
"What skills does this project demonstrate so far?"
```

## Mini Project Checkpoint — Foundation Complete

By the end of today, you should have:

Clean file structure

Semantic HTML

Base CSS styling

JavaScript connected

A clear plan for dynamic content

If yes — you're on track.

## Knowledge Check (ReflectionBased)

Answer:

a. What part felt most solid?

b. What part felt uncertain?

c. What do you want to improve tomorrow?

## Chapter WrapUp

Today you:

Planned a real project

Built strong foundations

Applied layout and design skills

Prepared for dynamic behavior

## Day 22 Preview

Project 1: Dynamic Content with JavaScript (Part 2)

Tomorrow, you'll:

- Generate content from data
- Create elements dynamically
- Bring your project to life

# 22

# Project 1: Dynamic Content with JavaScript (Part 2)

**Day 22 of 30**

## Learning Objectives

By the end of this chapter, you will be able to:

- Store structured content using arrays and objects
- Dynamically generate HTML content with JavaScript
- Separate data, logic, and DOM rendering clearly
- Create reusable render functions
- Update the page by changing data—not HTML
- Debug dynamic content confidently
- Use AI prompts to reason about architecture and flow

## Vibe Learning Mindset (Chapter Focus)

"Data drives the interface." Modern websites don't have hardcode content. They **render views from data**. Once this clicks, you stop "editing HTML" and start **building systems**.

## What You're Building Today

You'll complete the **dynamic core** of your personal website by:

- Defining your content in JavaScript

- Generating sections dynamically
- Rendering lists cleanly and predictably

By the end of today, **changing data will automatically update the page.**

# 1. Defining Your Project Data

Open `script.js`.

This is where your content will live.

## Example: Topics Data (Array of Objects)

```
const topics = [
  {
    title: "HTML",
    description: "Structure and meaning of web pages"
  },
  {
    title: "CSS",
    description: "Layout, design, and visual styling"
  },
  {
    title: "JavaScript",
    description: "Logic, interaction, and dynamic behavior"
  }
];
```

Why objects?

- Each topic has multiple properties
- Data is easy to expand later

## Exercise 1 — Personalize the Data

Replace the sample content with:

- Your own topics
- Your own descriptions

No DOM changes yet.

## 2. Identifying the Render Target

Back in `index.html`, you already planned this section:

```
<section id="topics">
  <h2>What I'm Learning</h2>
</section>
```

This section will become **datadriven.**

### Select the Container

```
const topicsSection = document.querySelector("#topics");
```

### Exercise 2 — Selection Check

Log `topicsSection` to the console.Confirm it exists.

## 3. Creating a Render Function (Core Pattern)

Instead of writing DOM code everywhere, create a **single function.**

```
function renderTopics() {
  // rendering logic will live here
}
```

Why this matters:

- Cleaner code
- Reusable logic
- Easier debugging

## 4. Rendering One Topic (StepbyStep)

Inside `renderTopics()`:

```
function renderTopics() {
  topics.forEach(function (topic) {
    const article = document.createElement("article");
    const title = document.createElement("h3");
    const desc = document.createElement("p");
    title.textContent = topic.title;
    desc.textContent = topic.description;
    article.appendChild(title);
```

```
    article.appendChild(desc);
    topicsSection.appendChild(article);
  });
}
```

## Call the Function

```
renderTopics();
```

Refresh the page.

🎉 Your content is now **generated by JavaScript**.

## Exercise 3 — Verify the Flow

Change:

- A title
- A description

Refresh the page.Observe automatic updates.

# 5. Styling the Dynamic Content

Add to `styles.css`:

```
#topics article {
  background: white;
  padding: 20px;
  marginbottom: 20px;
  borderradius: 6px;
}
```

Dynamic elements behave just like static ones.

## Exercise 4 — Visual Polish

Adjust:

- Padding
- Spacing
- Background color

Make the section feel intentional.

## 6. Clearing Content Before ReRendering (Important!)

If you rerender later, you must clear old content.

At the top of `renderTopics()`:

```
topicsSection.innerHTML = "<h2>What I'm Learning</h2>";
```

Now the section resets before rebuilding.

### Why This Matters

Without clearing:

- Content duplicates
- Bugs appear
- Logic becomes confusing

### Exercise 5 — Rebuild Test

Call `renderTopics()` twice.Confirm content does not duplicate.

## 7. Separating Responsibilities (Professional Habit)

Think in **roles:**

- Data → topics
- Logic → renderTopics()
- Structure → HTML
- Style → CSS

This separation makes projects:

- Easier to maintain
- Easier to extend
- Easier to debug

## 8. Refactoring for Readability

Optional improvement:

```
function createTopicCard(topic) {
  const article = document.createElement("article");
  const title = document.createElement("h3");
```

```
  const desc = document.createElement("p");
  title.textContent = topic.title;
  desc.textContent = topic.description;
  article.append(title, desc);
  return article;
}
```

Then:

```
function renderTopics() {
  topicsSection.innerHTML = "<h2>What I'm Learning</h2>";
  topics.forEach(function (topic) {
    topicsSection.appendChild(createTopicCard(topic));
  });
}
```

### Exercise 6 — Refactor

Extract one piece of logic into a helper function.

## 9. Debugging Dynamic Content

If nothing appears:

a. Check the console
b. Confirm function is called
c. Confirm container exists
d. Confirm data is not empty

Debug the **flow**, not just the code.

## 10. Common Beginner Dynamic Content Mistakes

### ❌ Mixing Data & DOM Everywhere

Keep rendering logic centralized.

### ❌ Hardcoding HTML Strings Too Early

Prefer `createElement()` for clarity.

### ❌ Forgetting to Clear Containers

This causes duplication bugs.

## 11. Learning Object — Data → View Flow

### Exercise 7 — Explain the Pipeline

Write one paragraph explaining:

- Where the data lives
- How it becomes HTML
- How the page updates

If you can explain it, you understand it.

## 12. MicroExperiments (Vibe Learning Core)

### Exercise 8 — Change the Data Only

Add a new topic object. Do **not** touch HTML or CSS.Refresh and observe.

### Exercise 9 — Change the Layout

Wrap articles in a grid or flex container.Observe how layout adapts.

## AI Prompts (Chapter 22)

### Prompt 1 — Architecture Review

```
"Review my datadriven rendering approach and suggest improvements."
```

### Prompt 2 — Debugging Partner

```
"My dynamic content isn't rendering. Ask me questions to diagnose it."
```

### Prompt 3 — Refactoring Advice

```
"How can I make this rendering code more reusable?"
```

### Prompt 4 — Mental Model

```
"Explain datadriven UI rendering in simple terms."
```

## Mini Project Checkpoint — Dynamic Core Complete

By the end of today, you should have:

Content defined as data

JavaScriptgenerated HTML

Clean render functions

Styled dynamic elements

Clear separation of concerns

This is **real frontend development.**

## Knowledge Check (ReflectionBased)

Answer:

- What part of the render process finally clicked?
- What felt most powerful today?
- What would be hard to do without this approach?

## Chapter WrapUp

Today you:

Rendered content from data

Built reusable DOM logic

Applied professional structure

Leveled up from static pages

## Day 23 Preview

Project 1: Interactivity & User Controls (Part 3)

Tomorrow you'll:

- Add buttons and interactions
- Filter or modify displayed content

# 23

# Project 1: Interactivity & User Controls (Part 3)

**Day 23 of 30**

## Learning Objectives

By the end of this chapter, you will be able to:

- Add interactive controls (buttons, inputs) to a real project
- Respond to user actions using events and logic
- Filter or modify displayed content dynamically
- Rerender content safely based on user input
- Maintain clean separation between data, logic, and DOM
- Prevent common interactivity bugs
- Use AI prompts to reason about UX and interaction flow

## Vibe Learning Mindset (Chapter Focus)

"Interactivity gives users agency." Static sites *tell*. Dynamic sites *respond*.

Interactive sites *listen*.

Your job is to make interaction **clear, safe, and predictable**.

## What You're Building Today

You'll enhance your personal website so users can:

- Interact with buttons
- Change what content is displayed
- See immediate feedback

By the end of today, your site will feel **alive and responsive to user intent.**

## 1. Defining the Interaction Goal

Before coding, ask:

- What can the user control?
- What should change when they interact?
- What stays the same?

### Example Interaction Ideas

a. Show only certain topics

b. Highlight a selected topic

c. Toggle visibility

d. Reset the view

### Exercise 1 — Interaction Planning

Write down **one clear interaction**, for example: "When the user clicks a button, only JavaScript topics are shown." Keep it simple.

## 2. Adding Controls to the HTML

Open `index.html`.

Add a controls area **above** the dynamic content:

```
<section id="controls">
  <button datafilter="all">All</button>
  <button datafilter="HTML">HTML</button>
  <button datafilter="CSS">CSS</button>
  <button datafilter="JavaScript">JavaScript</button>
</section>
```

Why `datafilter`?

- Stores intent directly in HTML
- Keeps JavaScript clean

### Exercise 2 — Customize Controls

Adjust:

- Button labels
- Filter values
- Number of buttons

## 3. Styling the Controls (Usability First)

In `styles.css`:

```
#controls {
  marginbottom: 30px;
}
#controls button {
  marginright: 10px;
  padding: 8px 14px;
  cursor: pointer;
}
```

Buttons should:

- Look clickable
- Be easy to tap
- Feel consistent

### Exercise 3 — Visual Feedback

Add a hover style to buttons.

## 4. Listening for User Interaction

In `script.js`, select the buttons:

```
const buttons = document.querySelectorAll("#controls button");
```

## Add Event Listeners

```
buttons.forEach(function (button) {
  button.addEventListener("click", function () {
    const filter = button.dataset.filter;
    handleFilter(filter);
  });
});
```

Read this as:

"When a button is clicked, figure out what filter it represents."

## Exercise 4 — Console Check

Log the `filter` value on click. Confirm correct behavior.

## 5. Creating the Filter Logic

Add a function:

```
function handleFilter(filter) {
  if (filter === "all") {
    renderTopics(topics);
  } else {
    const filtered = topics.filter(function (topic) {
      return topic.title === filter;
    });
    renderTopics(filtered);
  }
}
```

## Update renderTopics

Modify it to accept data:

```
function renderTopics(list) {
  topicsSection.innerHTML = "<h2>What I'm Learning</h2>";
  list.forEach(function (topic) {
    topicsSection.appendChild(createTopicCard(topic));
  });
}
```

## Initial Render

```
renderTopics(topics);
```

## Exercise 5 — Filter Test

Click each button. Confirm content updates correctly.

# 6. Why This Pattern Matters

This pattern separates:

- What happened (button click)
- What it means (filter value)
- What changes (rendered data)

This is **professionallevel thinking**, even in beginner code.

# 7. Adding Active State Feedback (UX Improvement)

In CSS:

```
#controls button.active {
  background: #333;
  color: white;
}
```

## Update JavaScript

```
function updateActiveButton(activeButton) {
  buttons.forEach(btn => btn.classList.remove("active"));
  activeButton.classList.add("active");
}
```

Call it inside the click handler:

```
updateActiveButton(button);
```

## Exercise 6 — Visual Confirmation

Ensure the active filter is clearly visible.

## 8. Guarding Against Edge Cases

What if:

- No items match?
- Data is empty?

Add a check in `renderTopics`:

```
if (list.length === 0) {
  topicsSection.innerHTML += "<p>No topics found.</p>";
  return;
}
```

### Exercise 7 — Edge Case Test

Temporarily filter for something that doesn't exist. Confirm graceful behavior.

## 9. Common Beginner Interactivity Mistakes

### ❌ Hardcoding Conditions

Use datadriven logic instead.

### ❌ Rebuilding HTML Without Clearing

Always reset containers before rendering.

### ❌ Mixing Click Logic with Rendering Logic

Keep responsibilities separate.

## 10. Learning Object — Interaction Flow Map

### Exercise 8 — Flow Explanation

Write out:

- User clicks
- Filter value read
- Data filtered
- Content rendered

If this makes sense — your architecture is solid.

# 11. MicroExperiments (Vibe Learning Core)

## Exercise 9 — Change the Interaction

Modify:

- Filter condition
- Button behavior
- Default view

Observe how logic adapts.

## Exercise 10 — Add One Control

Add a new button:

- "Beginner Only"
- "Core Topics"
- "Reset"

Implement behavior.

# AI Prompts (Chapter 23)

## Prompt 1 — UX Review

```
"Review this interaction flow and suggest UX improvements."
```

## Prompt 2 — Debugging Help

```
"My filter buttons aren't working. Ask me questions to diagnose the
issue."
```

## Prompt 3 — Code Quality

```
"How can I simplify or improve this eventhandling logic?"
```

## Prompt 4 — Feature Ideas

```
"What beginnerfriendly interactive features could I add next?"
```

## Mini Project Checkpoint — Interactive Project Complete

By the end of today, you should have:

User controls

Eventdriven logic

Filtered rendering

Visual feedback

Graceful edge handling

This is real, interactive frontend development.

## Knowledge Check (ReflectionBased)

Answer:

- What part of interactivity felt hardest?
- What pattern felt reusable?
- How does this improve user experience?

## Chapter WrapUp

Today you:

Added meaningful interactivity

Connected UI controls to data

Improved UX with feedback

Completed Project 1

## Day 24 Preview

Debugging, Errors & Developer Tools: Thinking Like a Developer

Next, you'll learn how developers **find, understand, and fix problems** efficiently — a critical professional skill.

# 24

# Debugging, Errors & Developer Tools: Thinking Like a Developer

**Day 24 of 30**

## Learning Objectives

By the end of this chapter, you will be able to:

- Explain what debugging really is (and why it's normal)
- Identify common types of JavaScript, HTML, and CSS errors
- Use the browser's Developer Tools confidently
- Read error messages without panic
- Debug problems systematically instead of guessing
- Understand the difference between bugs and bad logic
- Use AI prompts as a debugging partner, not a crutch

## Vibe Learning Mindset (Chapter Focus)

"Bugs are not failures — they're feedback."

Every developer:

- Breaks things
- Sees errors
- Gets confused

The difference is **how they respond**. Debugging is not about being smart — it's about being **methodical**.

## What You're Building Today

You're building something invisible but critical:

- Confidence
- Problemsolving skills
- Developer thinking habits

By the end of today, errors will feel **manageable**, not scary.

## 1. What Is Debugging (Really)?

Debugging is the process of:

- Finding why something isn't working
- Understanding what the code is actually doing
- Fixing the root cause

Debugging is **not**:

- Guessing
- Randomly changing code
- Rewriting everything

### RealWorld Analogy

If a lamp doesn't turn on, you:

- Check if it's plugged in
- Check the bulb
- Check the switch

You don't replace the house.

## 2. The Developer Tools (DevTools)

Every modern browser has **Developer Tools**.

Open them by:

- Rightclick → Inspect
- Or F12
- Or Cmd + Option + I (Mac)

## The Four Panels You'll Use Most

- Elements → HTML & CSS
- Console → JavaScript messages & errors
- Sources → JavaScript files
- Network → (later) loading & data

Today, we focus on **Elements** and **Console**.

# 3. The Console: Your Debugging Hub

The console shows:

- Logs (console.log)
- Errors
- Warnings

## Example Error Message

```
Uncaught TypeError: Cannot read properties of null
```

This means:

- JavaScript tried to use something
- But it didn't exist
- But it didn't exist

This is **information**, not judgment.

## Exercise 1 — Console Comfort

Open the console and:

- Log a message
- Create a fake error on purpose
- Observe how it appears

## 4. Using console.log() Strategically

`console.log()` is your flashlight.

Bad use:

```
console.log("hello");
```

Good use:

```
console.log("Button clicked");
console.log(userInput);
console.log(topics.length);
```

### Debugging Pattern

- Log before the problem
- Log inside the logic
- Log after the logic

Find where behavior changes.

### Exercise 2 — Trace the Flow

Add logs to:

- An event listener
- A function
- A conditional

Read the output like a story.

## 5. Common JavaScript Errors (BeginnerFriendly)

### ❌ ReferenceError

```
x is not defined
```

Meaning:

- Variable doesn't exist
- Typo or scope issue

### ❌ TypeError

```
Cannot read properties of null
```

Meaning:

- Element wasn't found
- DOM selector failed

## ❌ SyntaxError

```
Unexpected token
```

Meaning:

- Missing bracket
- Extra comma
- Broken structure

### Exercise 3 — Error Recognition

Match:

- Error type
- Likely cause
- Where to look first

## 6. Debugging DOM Issues

### Problem: Element Is null

```
document.querySelector("#topics");
```

Possible causes:

- ID doesn't exist
- Script runs before HTML loads
- Typo in selector

### Fix Checklist

- Check HTML spelling
- Check selector
- Check script placement

### Exercise 4 — DOM Debug

Break a selector on purpose.

Read the error. Fix it.

## 7. Debugging Logic Errors (Hardest Kind)

Sometimes code runs — but does the wrong thing.

Example:

```
if (age > 18) {
  console.log("Adult");
}
```

What about age = 18?

This is not a syntax bug — it's a **logic bug**.

### Logic Debug Strategy

Ask:

- What should happen?
- What is happening?
- Where do they differ?

### Exercise 5 — Logic Check

Change a condition.

Predict behavior. Test it.

## 8. Using the Elements Panel (Visual Debugging)

The **Elements** tab lets you:

- Inspect HTML
- See applied CSS
- Toggle styles on/off

### Powerful Trick

Uncheck CSS rules live to see impact.

### Exercise 6 — CSS Debug

Find an element and:

- Disable a margin
- Disable a display rule
- Observe layout changes

## 9. Breaking Things on Purpose (Safe Learning)

Good developers **experiment safely.**

Try:

- Removing a closing tag
- Renaming a class
- Commenting out code

Then fix it.

### Exercise 7 — Controlled Break

Break:

- One HTML rule
- One CSS rule
- One JS line

Fix each intentionally.

## 10. Debugging Checklist (Beginner Gold)

When something doesn't work:

- Check the console
- Read the error message
- Locate the file + line number
- Add console.log()
- Verify assumptions
- Fix one thing at a time

Never change everything at once.

## 11. Learning Object — Think Like a Detective

### Exercise 8 — Debug Narrative

Write:

- What you expected
- What happened instead

- What you checked
- What fixed it

This builds **debugging memory**.

# 12. MicroExperiments (Vibe Learning Core)

## Exercise 9 — Silent Failure

Write code that:

Runs

Does nothing

Figure out *why*.

## Exercise 10 — Error Reading

Copy an error message. Explain it in your own words.

# AI Prompts (Chapter 24)

## Prompt 1 — Error Translation

```
"Explain this JavaScript error message in plain English."
```

## Prompt 2 — Debugging Coach

```
"Ask me stepbystep questions to help debug this issue."
```

## Prompt 3 — Logic Review

```
"Review this logic and point out potential edge cases."
```

## Prompt 4 — Debug Strategy

```
"What's the best way to debug this type of problem?"
```

# Mini Project — Debugging Practice Session

## Exercise 11

Intentionally introduce:

- One JavaScript error
- One DOM error
- One logic error

Then:

- Identify each
- Explain the cause
- Fix it cleanly

Document your process in comments.

## Knowledge Check (ReflectionBased)

Answer:

- Which error type feels least scary now?
- What debugging step helped the most?
- How has your mindset changed?

## Chapter WrapUp

Today you:

Learned how developers debug

Used DevTools effectively

Read errors calmly

Built confidence and resilience

## Day 25 Preview

Project 2: Polishing, Refactoring & Code Quality

You'll clean, improve, and professionalize your code — the difference between *working* and *wellbuilt.*

# 25

# Project 2: Polishing, Refactoring & Code Quality

**Day 25 of 30**

## Learning Objectives

By the end of this chapter, you will be able to:

- Explain what "code quality" means in practical terms
- Identify messy, fragile, or unclear code
- Refactor JavaScript safely without breaking behavior
- Improve naming, structure, and readability
- Apply consistency across HTML, CSS, and JavaScript
- Understand the difference between "working code" and "good code"
- Use AI prompts as a code review assistant, not an autowriter

## Vibe Learning Mindset (Chapter Focus)

"Professional code is written for humans first." Browsers don't care how messy your code is.

**People do** — including future you.

Refactoring is not punishment. It's **respect for your work**.

## What You're Building Today

You're not adding new features today.

Instead, you are:

- Improving clarity
- Reducing confusion
- Strengthening what already exists

By the end of today, your project will feel **calm, readable, and intentional.**

## 1. What Is Refactoring?

Refactoring means:

Changing the *structure* of code without changing its *behavior*.

You are:

- Not adding features
- Not fixing bugs
- Improving how the code is written

### Before vs After Mindset

✘ "It works, don't touch it & "It works, let's make it better"

## 2. Signs Code Needs Refactoring

Look for these signals:

- Repeated code
- Long functions doing too much
- Confusing variable names
- Mixed responsibilities
- Hardtofollow logic

### Exercise 1 — Refactor Radar

Open your project and mark:

- One confusing section
- One repeated pattern
- One "I forgot why I wrote this" area

## 3. Naming: The Biggest Quality Upgrade

Bad names create confusion.

### Weak Names

```
let x;
function doThing() {}
```

### Strong Names

```
let activeFilter;
function renderTopics() {}
```

Code should explain itself without comments.

### Exercise 2 — Rename for Clarity

Rename:

- One variable
- One function
- One DOM selector reference

Confirm nothing breaks.

## 4. One Function = One Job

### Problem Example

```
function handleClick() {
  // filter data
  // update DOM
  // log output
}
```

This function does **too much.**

### Better Structure

```
function handleFilterClick() {}
function filterTopics() {}
function renderTopics() {}
```

Each function has **one responsibility.**

### Exercise 3 — Split a Function

Find one long function. Split it into 2–3 smaller ones.

## 5. Refactoring Without Fear (Safe Process)

Follow this order:

- Identify one improvement
- Change only that
- Refresh and test
- Move on

Never refactor *everything* at once.

### Exercise 4 — Safe Refactor

Refactor one small thing. Test. Stop.

This builds trust in yourself.

## 6. Cleaning Up JavaScript Structure

### Group Related Code

```
// Data
const topics = [...]
// DOM references
const topicsSection = ...
// Rendering functions
function renderTopics() {}
// Event handlers
function handleFilter() {}
```

Order creates clarity.

### Exercise 5 — Reorder Code

Reorganize your JS file into logical sections.

No behavior changes allowed.

## 7. Improving HTML Readability

HTML should read like a document.

## Improve By:

- Consistent indentation
- Clear section grouping
- Semantic tags

## Exercise 6 — HTML Pass

Clean up:

- Indentation
- Spacing
- Section structure

# 8. Improving CSS Consistency

Look for:

- Repeated values
- Inconsistent spacing
- Random colors

## Refactor Example

Before:

```
marginbottom: 12px;
marginbottom: 16px;
marginbottom: 14px;
```

After:

```
marginbottom: 16px;
```

Consistency > creativity.

## Exercise 7 — CSS Cleanup

Standardize:

- Spacing
- Font sizes
- Colors

## 9. Comments: When & Why

Bad comments:

```
// this function runs
```

Good comments:

```
// Renders topic cards based on active filter
```

Comment *why*, not *what*.

### Exercise 8 — Comment Pass

Add one meaningful comment. Remove one useless comment.

## 10. Removing Dead Code

Dead code:

- Commentedout blocks
- Unused variables
- Old experiments

Dead code creates confusion.

### Exercise 9 — Code Pruning

Remove:

- One unused variable
- One commented block

Confirm nothing breaks.

## 11. Learning Object — Read Your Code Out Loud

### Exercise 10 — Human Read Test

Read one file out loud. If it sounds confusing — refactor.

Clarity is audible.

## 12. MicroExperiments (Vibe Learning Core)

### Exercise 11 — Refactor for Calm

Refactor one thing purely to make the file feel calmer.

No functional gain required.

### Exercise 12 — Compare Versions

Compare:

- Before refactor
- After refactor

Note what improved.

## AI Prompts (Chapter 25)

### Prompt 1 — Code Review

```
"Review this beginner JavaScript code and suggest readability
improvements."
```

### Prompt 2 — Refactor Advice

```
"How can I refactor this function to do one thing well?"
```

### Prompt 3 — Naming Help

```
"Suggest clearer variable and function names for this code."
```

### Prompt 4 — Professional Standards

```
"What would a professional developer improve in this code?"
```

## Mini Project — Code Quality Pass

### Exercise 13

Perform a **full quality pass** on your project:

- Rename unclear variables
- Split large functions
- Remove dead code
- Improve spacing and structure

Write a short summary of changes.

## Knowledge Check (ReflectionBased)

Answer:

- What refactor improved clarity the most?
- What felt risky but worked?
- How does your code feel now compared to yesterday?

## Chapter WrapUp

Today you:

Refactored safely

Improved readability

Applied professional habits

Strengthened your project

## Day 26 Preview

### Accessibility & Inclusive Web Design: Building for Everyone

You'll learn how to ensure your websites are usable by **all users**, not just some.

# 26

# Accessibility & Inclusive Web Design: Building for Everyone

**Day 26 of 30**

## Learning Objectives

By the end of this chapter, you will be able to:

- Explain what web accessibility is in clear, human terms
- Understand why accessibility matters ethically, legally, and professionally
- Apply basic accessibility principles to HTML, CSS, and JavaScript
- Use semantic HTML to improve screen reader support
- Design keyboardfriendly interactions
- Improve color contrast and text readability
- Use AI prompts to audit accessibility—not guess at it

## Vibe Learning Mindset (Chapter Focus)

"Accessibility is not a feature — it's a responsibility."

Accessible design is not about:

- Special users
- Extra effort
- Advanced techniques

It's about **not excluding people by accident.**

## What You're Building Today

You're upgrading your project so it is:

- Easier to read
- Easier to navigate
- Usable with keyboard and assistive tools

By the end of today, your website will be **more human friendly** — for everyone.

## 1. What Is Web Accessibility?

Web accessibility means:

People with different abilities can **perceive, understand, navigate, and interact** with your website.

This includes people who:

- Use screen readers
- Navigate by keyboard
- Have low vision or color blindness
- Have motor or cognitive differences

Accessibility improves usability for **all users**, not just some.

## 2. Why Accessibility Matters

### Ethical

The web should be usable by everyone.

### Legal

Many countries require accessibility compliance (WCAG based laws).

### Professional

Accessible developers are **better developers**.

Accessibility is a sign of quality, not limitation.

# 3. Semantic HTML = Accessibility for Free

Semantic HTML gives meaning to structure.

## Good Example

```
<header>
  <nav>
    <main>
      <section>
        <footer>
```

## Bad Example

```
<div>
  <div>
    <div>
```

Screen readers rely on **meaning**, not appearance.

## Exercise 1 — Semantic Audit

Review your HTML and ask:

- Is this a header, nav, main, section, or footer?
- Am I using <div> where a semantic tag fits better?

Improve one section.

# 4. Headings & Content Structure

Headings create a **content outline**.

Rules:

- One <h1> per page
- Headings should be in order
- Don't skip levels for styling

## Good Structure

```
<h1>Page Title</h1>
<h2>Section</h2>
<h3>Subsection</h3>
```

### Exercise 2 — Heading Check

Scan your page:

- Are headings logical?
- Can content be understood by headings alone?

Fix where needed.

## 5. Accessible Text & Readability

Accessibility includes:

- Font size
- Line height
- Contrast

### Recommended Defaults

```
body {
  fontsize: 16px;
  lineheight: 1.6;
}
```

### Color Contrast Rule (BeginnerFriendly)

If text is hard to read — it's not accessible.

### Exercise 3 — Readability Test

View your site in:

- Bright light
- Low brightness

Improve contrast where needed.

## 6. Links & Buttons (Meaning Matters)

### ❌ Bad

```
<a href="#">Click here</a>
```

### Good

```
<a href="#">View course topics</a>
```

Screen readers read links **out of context**.

## Exercise 4 — Link Language

Improve the wording of:

- One link
- One button

Make intent clear.

# 7. Keyboard Accessibility (Critical!)

Many users navigate **without a mouse**.

## Test This:

- Use Tab to move through your site
- Use Enter to activate buttons

If you can't navigate — it's not accessible.

## Exercise 5 — Keyboard Navigation

Navigate your site using only:

- Tab
- Shift + Tab
- Enter

Fix any dead ends.

# 8. Focus Styles (Do Not Remove!)

Browsers show focus outlines for a reason.

❌ Don't do this:

```
outline: none;
```

Do this instead:

```
:focus {
  outline: 2px solid #333;
}
```

### Exercise 6 — Focus Visibility

Ensure focused elements are **clearly visible**.

## 9. Forms & Labels (Accessibility Essential)

Every input needs a label.

### Good

```
<label for="email">Email</label>
<input id="email" type="email">
```

Placeholder text is **not** a replacement.

### Exercise 7 — Form Audit

Check:

- Inputs
- Labels
- Button clarity

Fix one issue.

## 10. Accessible JavaScript Interactions

JavaScript should:

- Respect keyboard interaction
- Not rely only on mouse events

### Example

If something is clickable:

- It should be focusable
- It should work with Enter

### Exercise 8 — Interaction Test

Test one JS feature:

- With mouse
- With keyboard

Ensure both work.

## 11. Common Accessibility Mistakes

### ❌ Using Color Alone to Convey Meaning

Add text or icons.

### ❌ Skipping Heading Levels

Breaks screen reader navigation.

### ❌ Removing Focus Styles

Disorients keyboard users.

## 12. Learning Object — Accessibility Mindset Shift

### Exercise 9 — Empathy Check

Ask:

- What if I couldn't see this?
- What if I couldn't use a mouse?
- What if I relied on audio?

Adjust one design choice accordingly.

## 13. MicroExperiments (Vibe Learning Core)

### Exercise 10 — Screen Reader Awareness

Rightclick → Inspect → hover HTML nodes

Observe how structure matters.

### Exercise 11 — Accessibility Improvement Log

Write down:

- One accessibility issue you fixed
- Why it mattered
- Who it helps

## AI Prompts (Chapter 26)

### Prompt 1 — Accessibility Audit

```
"Review this beginner website for accessibility issues and suggest
improvements."
```

### Prompt 2 — Inclusive Design

```
"How can I make this interaction more inclusive for keyboard users?"
```

### Prompt 3 — Contrast Check

```
"Does this color combination meet accessibility contrast guidelines?"
```

### Prompt 4 — Learning Reinforcement

```
"Explain accessibility in a way I can explain to a nondeveloper."
```

## Mini Project — Accessibility Upgrade Pass

### Exercise 12

Perform an accessibility pass on your project:

- Improve semantics
- Fix heading structure
- Improve contrast
- Test keyboard navigation

Document your changes.

## Knowledge Check (ReflectionBased)

Answer:

- What accessibility improvement surprised you?
- What felt easiest to fix?
- How does this change how you see web design?

## Chapter WrapUp

Today you:

Learned what accessibility really means

Improved inclusivity and usability

Applied ethical design principles

Became a more responsible developer

## Day 27 Preview

**Performance, Optimization & Best Practices: Making Websites Fast & Smooth**

# 27

# Performance, Optimization & Best Practices: Making Websites Fast & Smooth

**Day 27 of 30**

## Learning Objectives

By the end of this chapter, you will be able to:

- Explain what web performance actually means (beyond "speed")
- Identify common performance issues in beginner projects
- Write more efficient HTML, CSS, and JavaScript
- Reduce unnecessary work in the browser
- Understand when optimization matters—and when it doesn't
- Apply practical best practices used by professionals
- Use AI prompts to analyze and optimize, not overengineer

## Vibe Learning Mindset (Chapter Focus)

"Fast websites feel trustworthy." Performance is not about chasing perfect scores. It's about **respecting the user's time, device, and attention.**

Good performance is mostly about **not doing unnecessary work.**

## What You're Building Today

You're improving your project so it:

- Loads quickly
- Responds smoothly
- Feels intentional and polished

By the end of today, your site will feel **lighter, calmer, and more professional.**

## 1. What Does "Performance" Mean?

Performance includes:

- Load speed (how fast the page appears)
- Responsiveness (how quickly it reacts)
- Smoothness (no jank or freezing)
- Efficiency (not wasting resources)

Performance is about **experience**, not just numbers.

## 2. Beginner Truth: Most Performance Problems Are SelfInflicted

Common causes:

- Too much JavaScript running unnecessarily
- Rebuilding the DOM repeatedly
- Overcomplex CSS
- Large images
- Doing work more often than needed

The fix is usually **simplification.**

## 3. HTML Performance Best Practices

### Keep HTML Clean & Semantic

Semantic HTML:

- Loads efficiently
- Is easier to parse
- Helps browsers optimize rendering

Avoid:

- Deeply nested <div>s
- Unnecessary wrappers

## Exercise 1 — HTML Simplification

Remove:

- One unnecessary wrapper
- One redundant element

Confirm layout still works.

# 4. CSS Performance & Simplicity

CSS is fast by default — unless you fight it.

## Best Practices

- Prefer simple selectors
- Avoid overly specific rules
- Reuse classes instead of duplicating styles

## Example

❌ Too complex:

```
main section div article p span { }
```

Simple:

```
.cardtext { }
```

## Exercise 2 — CSS Cleanup

Refactor one complex selector into a reusable class.

# 5. JavaScript Performance: Do Less, Not Faster

## Key Principle

```
The fastest code is the code you don't run.
```

Avoid:

- Running code on every resize or scroll
- Rerendering everything when only part changes
- Repeating DOM queries unnecessarily

## Cache DOM References

❌ Bad:

```
document.querySelector("#topics");
document.querySelector("#topics");
```

Good:

```
const topicsSection = document.querySelector("#topics");
```

## Exercise 3 — JS Efficiency Pass

Find one repeated DOM query and cache it.

# 6. Smarter Rendering (Critical for Dynamic Content)

Avoid rebuilding content if nothing changed.

## Example Thought Process

- Did the data change?
- If not, don't rerender
- If yes, update only what's needed

Beginner win: **Rerender only on user action**, not constantly.

## Exercise 4 — Render Discipline

Ensure `renderTopics()` is only called:

- On page load
- On filter change

Not elsewhere.

## 7. Images & Assets (BeginnerFriendly)

Large images slow sites down more than code.

### Best Practices

- Resize images before using them
- Don't rely on CSS to shrink huge files
- Use appropriate formats (JPG, PNG, SVG)

### Exercise 5 — Image Check

If your project uses images:

- Confirm size is reasonable
- Replace one oversized image if needed

## 8. Perceived Performance (Huge UX Win)

Sometimes it's not about actual speed —it's about **what the user feels.**

Examples:

- Immediate feedback on click
- Loading messages
- Disabled buttons while processing

### Exercise 6 — Feedback Improvement

Add:

- A visual response on button click
- A short message during updates

This increases trust.

## 9. Measuring Performance (BeginnerLevel)

Use:

- Browser DevTools → Performance (optional)
- Network tab to see load timing
- Your own eyes (seriously)

If it *feels* slow, it probably is.

### Exercise 7 — Load Awareness

Reload your page with DevTools open.

Observe:

- What loads first
- What loads last

## 10. Common Beginner Performance Mistakes

### ❌ Premature Optimization

Don't optimize imaginary problems.

### ❌ Copying Advanced Patterns Too Early

Simple code often performs better.

### ❌ Ignoring Mobile Devices

Lowpower devices reveal issues faster.

## 11. Learning Object — Performance Thinking

### Exercise 8 — Cost Awareness

Ask of each feature:

- How often does this run?
- Does it need to?
- What happens on slow devices?

Remove one unnecessary action.

## 12. MicroExperiments (Vibe Learning Core)

### Exercise 9 — Remove One Thing

Remove one feature temporarily. Does the site feel faster or calmer?

### Exercise 10 — Refactor for Less Work

Refactor one function to:

- Run fewer times
- Do less inside

Test behavior.

## AI Prompts (Chapter 27)

### Prompt 1 — Performance Review

```
"Review this beginner project and suggest simple performance
improvements."
```

### Prompt 2 — Optimization Strategy

```
"What performance issues should I worry about at my skill level?"
```

### Prompt 3 — Code Simplification

```
"How can I simplify this code to improve performance?"
```

### Prompt 4 — UX Feedback

```
"How can I improve perceived performance for users?"
```

## Mini Project — Performance Optimization Pass

### Exercise 11

Perform a performance pass on your project:

- Cache DOM references
- Reduce unnecessary renders
- Simplify CSS selectors
- Improve user feedback

Write a short summary of what you improved and why.

## Knowledge Check (ReflectionBased)

Answer:

- What performance improvement was easiest?
- What surprised you about performance?
- How does optimization relate to empathy for users?

## Chapter WrapUp

Today you:

Improved performance intentionally

Reduced unnecessary work

Applied professional best practices

Made your site feel smoother

## Day 28 Preview

### Deployment & Publishing: Putting Your Website Online

You'll learn how to take your project from your computer to the **real web** — a huge confidence milestone.

# 28

# Deployment & Publishing: Putting Your Website Online

**Day 28 of 30**

## Learning Objectives

By the end of this chapter, you will be able to:

- Explain what "deployment" means in plain language
- Understand how websites are hosted and accessed
- Prepare a project for public viewing
- Publish a static website using a beginnerfriendly platform
- Troubleshoot common deployment issues
- Share your website confidently with others
- Use AI prompts to validate and prepare deployments safely

## Vibe Learning Mindset (Chapter Focus)

"A website isn't real until someone else can see it."

Deployment is not advanced. It's simply the step where your files become **publicly accessible.**

This is where learning turns into **confidence**.

## What You're Building Today

You are publishing your **first real website**.

By the end of today, you will have:

- A live URL
- A public version of your project
- Proof that you can ship

This matters more than perfection.

## 1. What Is Deployment?

**Deployment** means:

Uploading your website files to a server so others can access them via the internet.

Your browser:

- Requests files from a server
- The server sends HTML, CSS, and JavaScript
- The browser displays the page

Deployment puts your files where browsers can find them.

## 2. What Makes a Site "Deployable"?

Your project is deployable if:

It uses static files (`.html`, `.css`, `.js`)

File paths are correct

Everything runs locally without errors

Good news: Your project already qualifies.

## 3. Final PreDeployment Checklist

Before publishing, confirm:

- No console errors
- All links work
- All files are referenced correctly
- No absolute local paths (like C:\ or /Users/)

## Exercise 1 — PreFlight Check

Open your site locally and:

- Check the console
- Click everything
- Refresh once

Fix any visible issues.

## 4. BeginnerFriendly Hosting Options

There are many hosting platforms. For beginners, the best are **simple, free, and safe.**

### Recommended Options

- GitHub Pages
- Netlify
- Vercel

Today, we'll focus on **GitHub Pages** because:

- It's free
- It's widely used
- It builds professional habits

## 5. Preparing Your Files for GitHub Pages

Your project should look like this:

```
project/
├─ index.html
├─ styles.css
└─ script.js
```

Important:

- The main file must be named index.html
- File names are casesensitive

## Exercise 2 — File Name Audit

Confirm:

- index.html spelling
- Matching file references
- No extra spaces or capitalization mismatches

# 6. Publishing with GitHub Pages (Conceptual Steps)

You don't need to master Git today — just understand the flow.

## HighLevel Process

- Create a GitHub account
- Create a new repository
- Upload your project files
- Enable GitHub Pages
- Visit your live URL

## What GitHub Pages Does

- Hosts your files
- Serves them publicly
- Updates automatically when files change

# 7. Common Deployment Issues (BeginnerSafe)

## ❌ Page Loads but Looks Broken

Cause:

CSS file not linked correctly

Fix:

Check `<link href="styles.css">`

## ❌ JavaScript Not Running

Cause:

- Script path incorrect
- Script placed incorrectly

Fix:

```
<script src="script.js"></script>
```

Place it **before *</body>***.

## ❌ 404 Errors

Cause:

- File name mismatch
- Case sensitivity issue

Fix:

- Match file names exactly

## Exercise 3 — Intentional Mistake

Break a file path on purpose.

Observe the result. Fix it.

This builds confidence.

## 8. Testing the Live Site

Once deployed:

- Open the live URL
- Refresh multiple times
- Test on a different browser
- Test on mobile if possible

Live environments reveal things local testing doesn't.

## Exercise 4 — Live Testing Checklist

Test:

- Navigation
- Buttons
- Dynamic content
- Keyboard navigation

Fix one live issue if found.

## 9. Understanding URLs & Structure

Your site URL will look like: `https://username.github.io/projectname/`

Key ideas:

- URL = address
- / matters
- Case matters

## 10. Updating a Live Website

To update:

- Change files
- Upload again
- Refresh the live site

Deployment is **iterative**, not onetime.

## 11. Learning Object — Shipping Mindset

### Exercise 5 — Version 1 Acceptance

Answer:

- What works?
- What could improve later?
- What are you proud of?

Shipping is progress.

## 12. MicroExperiments (Vibe Learning Core)

### Exercise 6 — Small Live Change

Change:

- Text
- Color
- Spacing

Upload again. Refresh the live site.

See the change in the real world.

## Exercise 7 — Share It

Share your URL with:

- A friend
- Yourself on another device
- A future version of you

This matters.

# AI Prompts (Chapter 28)

## Prompt 1 — Deployment Readiness

```
"Review my project and tell me if it's ready to deploy."
```

## Prompt 2 — Debugging Live Issues

```
"My site works locally but not live. Ask me questions to diagnose it."
```

## Prompt 3 — Portfolio Advice

```
"Is this project suitable as a beginner portfolio piece?"
```

## Prompt 4 — Next Steps

```
"What's a realistic next improvement for this deployed site?"
```

# Mini Project — Live Deployment

## Exercise 8

Deploy your website and document:

- The URL
- One issue you found
- One improvement you made after deployment

This is real developer work.

# Knowledge Check (ReflectionBased)

Answer:

- How did it feel to see your site live?
- What surprised you about deployment?
- What would you improve next?

## Chapter WrapUp

Today you:

Deployed a real websit

Learned how hosting works

Fixed live issues

Crossed a major milestone

## Day 29 Preview

### Next Steps, Learning Paths & Building a Portfolio

You'll learn how to continue learning **without getting lost**, and how to turn this project into part of a growing portfolio.

# 29

# Next Steps, Learning Paths & Building a Portfolio

**Day 29 of 30**

## Learning Objectives

By the end of this chapter, you will be able to:

- Understand what "next steps" actually mean after learning the basics
- Identify realistic learning paths in web design and frontend development
- Turn your project into a portfolioready piece
- Recognize the difference between learning and progressing
- Avoid overwhelm and tutorial burnout
- Create a personal learning roadmap
- Use AI prompts to plan growth intentionally

## Vibe Learning Mindset (Chapter Focus)

"You don't need to learn everything — you need to learn *what's next.*"

Most beginners quit not because they can't learn —but because they don't know **where to focus.**

Clarity creates momentum.

## What You're Building Today

You're building:

- A direction
- A plan
- A portfolio mindset

By the end of today, you'll know how to keep growing **without guessing**.

## 1. The Beginner Plateau (And Why It's Normal)

After finishing a course, many learners feel:

- "I know some things, but not enough"
- "I don't feel jobready"
- "Everything looks advanced"

This is **normal.**

You are no longer a beginner —but not yet experienced.

This phase is called **early intermediate**, and it's where real growth happens.

## 2. What You Can Already Do (Reality Check)

You can already:

- Build a structured website
- Style layouts intentionally
- Use JavaScript for logic and interactivity
- Debug issues
- Deploy a site

That puts you ahead of most beginners.

### Exercise 1 — Skills Inventory

Write down:

- 5 things you can build now
- 3 things that felt hard but you completed

Confidence comes from evidence.

## 3. Learning Paths: Choosing Direction (Not Everything)

You don't need to learn *everything*. Choose a **path**.

### Common Beginner Paths

#### Web Design Focus

- Layout systems
- Responsive design
- Typography
- Design systems

#### FrontEnd Development Focus

- Deeper JavaScript
- APIs
- State & data flow
- Frameworks (later)

#### Hybrid (Most Common)

- Strong fundamentals
- Small interactive projects
- Gradual specialization

### Exercise 2 — Path Selection

Choose **one primary focus** for the next 30–60 days.

Write why.

## 4. Turning Your Project Into a Portfolio Piece

A portfolio project is not:

- Perfect
- Massive
- Advanced

It *is*:

- Clear
- Finished
- Explainable

### Portfolio Upgrade Checklist

Add:

- Clear heading
- Short description of the project
- What you learned
- What you'd improve next

### Exercise 3 — Project Description

Write a 4–5 sentence description of your project as if explaining it to a nondeveloper.

## 5. What Makes a Beginner Portfolio Strong

Recruiters and reviewers look for:

- Clean structure
- Intentional decisions
- Readable code
- Deployed projects

They do **not** expect:

- Framework mastery
- Perfect design
- Advanced algorithms

## 6. Avoiding Tutorial Hell

Tutorial hell is when you:

- Watch endlessly
- Don't build
- Don't struggle
- Don't finish

The fix:

Build small things without instructions.

## Exercise 4 — NoTutorial Challenge

Build a **tiny feature** without following a guide:

- Toggle content
- Filter data
- Add a new section

Google only when stuck.

# 7. How to Learn Effectively Going Forward

Follow this loop:

- Pick a small goal
- Try to build it
- Get stuck
- Debug
- Reflect
- Improve

Struggle is part of progress.

# 8. Expanding Your Skills (BeginnerSafe Topics)

Good next topics:

- Responsive design (media queries)
- Forms & validation
- Basic accessibility audits
- More JavaScript practice
- Working with real data

Avoid rushing into:

- Heavy frameworks
- Complex tooling
- Overengineering

## 9. Learning Object — Personal Roadmap

### Exercise 5 — 30Day Plan

Create a simple plan:

- 1 thing to improve weekly
- 1 project idea
- 1 concept to revisit

Keep it realistic.

## 10. Using AI as a Learning Partner (Not a Crutch)

AI should:

- Explain
- Ask questions
- Review code
- Suggest improvements

AI should not:

- Replace thinking
- Skip struggle
- Write everything for you

### Exercise 6 — AIAssisted Growth

Use AI to:

- Review your project
- Suggest next improvements
- Identify weak spots

Evaluate suggestions critically.

## 11. Confidence Comes From Repetition

You don't become confident by:

- Knowing more concepts
- Watching more videos

You become confident by:

- Building
- Fixing
- Finishing

## 12. MicroExperiments (Vibe Learning Core)

### Exercise 7 — Improve One Thing

Pick one improvement:

- UX
- Styling
- Performance
- Accessibility

Implement it today.

### Exercise 8 — Reflection Log

Write:

- What you learned this month
- What surprised you
- What you're excited to build next

This locks in growth.

## AI Prompts (Chapter 29)

### Prompt 1 — Learning Plan

```
"Help me create a realistic 30day learning plan based on my current
skills."
```

### Prompt 2 — Portfolio Review

```
"Review this beginner project and tell me how to improve it for a
portfolio."
```

### Prompt 3 — Direction Advice

```
"Based on my interests, what frontend path should I focus on next?"
```

## Prompt 4 — Confidence Check

```
"What evidence shows I'm making progress as a web developer?"
```

## Mini Project — Portfolio Prep

### Exercise 9

Prepare your project for sharing:

- Clean README or description
- Live URL
- Clear explanation

This is a real milestone.

## Knowledge Check (ReflectionBased)

Answer:

- What path excites you most?
- What will you build next?
- What are you proud of completing?

## Chapter WrapUp

Today you:

Gained clarity on next steps

Avoided common learning traps

Prepared a portfolio mindset

Built confidence through reflection

## Day 30 Preview

### Final Capstone, Reflection & Becoming a SelfDirected Web Designer

You'll:

- Reflect on your journey
- Solidify your identity as a builder
- Learn how to keep growing independently

# 30

# Final Capstone, Reflection & Becoming a Self-Directed Web Designer

Day 30 of 30

## Learning Objectives

By the end of this chapter, you will be able to:

- Complete a final capstone improvement to your project
- Reflect meaningfully on your 30day learning journey
- Identify how your thinking has changed since Day 1
- Understand what it means to be a selfdirected learner
- Build confidence based on evidence, not comparison
- Create a sustainable habit for continued growth
- Use AI prompts for lifelong learning support

## Vibe Learning Mindset (Chapter Focus)

"Learning to code was never the goal.

Learning how to *learn* was."

The most important skill you gained is not HTML, CSS, or JavaScript.

It is:

- Curiosity
- Problemsolving
- Persistence
- Selftrust

This chapter is about **owning that transformation**.

## What You're Building Today

You are building:

- A final, intentional improvement to your project
- A clear narrative of your learning journey
- A mindset shift from student → builder

By the end of today, you will no longer ask:

"Am I allowed to call myself a web designer?"

You already are one.

## 1. The Final Capstone (Small, Intentional, Finished)

Your capstone is **not** a new project.

It is: One meaningful improvement to your existing website.

### Choose ONE Improvement Area

Pick **one** (only one):

- Visual polish (spacing, colors, typography)
- Interactivity improvement
- Accessibility enhancement
- Performance optimization
- Code clarity / refactor

Small and finished beats ambitious and incomplete.

## Exercise 1 — Capstone Decision

Write:

- What you will improve
- Why this matters

How you'll know it's done

# 2. Implement the Improvement (Focused Build)

Work slowly and intentionally.

Guidelines:

- Change one thing at a time
- Test after each change
- Stop when the improvement is complete

## Exercise 2 — Build & Test

Implement your improvement.

Refresh.

Test with:

- Mouse
- Keyboard
- Console open

When it works, **stop**.

Finishing is the win.

# 3. Before & After Reflection (Evidence of Growth)

Open:

- Your Day 1 notes
- Your Day 30 project

Compare:

- Structure
- Confidence
- Clarity
- Problemsolving ability

### Exercise 3 — Before vs After

Write:

- What confused you on Day 1
- What feels obvious now
- What you can explain to others

Growth becomes real when you name it.

## 4. What You Actually Learned (Beyond Code)

You learned how to:

- Break problems into steps
- Debug without panic
- Learn independently
- Finish projects
- Trust yourself

These skills transfer **everywhere**.

## 5. The Shift to SelfDirected Learning

A selfdirected learner:

- Identifies gaps
- Experiments
- Reflects
- Adjusts
- Repeats

They don't wait for permission or perfect instructions.

## Exercise 4 — SelfDirected Proof

Write one example from this month where you:

- Figured something out
- Fixed something yourself
- Went beyond instructions

That's the shift.

## 6. Letting Go of Comparison

You may still think:

- "Others know more"
- "I'm not advanced enough"
- "I need one more course"

Reminder:

You are comparing your inside to others' outside.

Progress is personal.

## 7. Your New Identity: Builder, Not Beginner

You are no longer:

- "Just starting"
- "Trying to learn"
- "Watching tutorials"

You are:

- Building
- Shipping
- Improving
- Reflecting

That is what developers do.

## 8. Creating a Sustainable Learning Habit

The goal is not intensity — it's consistency.

Even:

- 20 minutes a day
- One small experiment
- One improvement per week

This compounds faster than motivation.

### Exercise 5 — Learning Habit Design

Choose:

- When you'll practice
- How often
- What "enough" looks like

Make it achievable.

## 9. Using AI for Lifelong Learning (The Right Way)

AI is now part of your toolkit.

Use it to:

- Explain concepts
- Review code
- Ask "what if?"
- Generate practice ideas

Never use it to:

- Skip thinking
- Avoid struggle
- Replace learning

## 10. Learning Object — Teach What You Learned

### Exercise 6 — Teaching Test

Explain one concept from this book:

- In writing
- Or out loud
- Or to an imaginary beginner

If you can teach it, you own it.

## 11. MicroExperiments (Vibe Learning Core)

### Exercise 7 — One Last Experiment

Change one small thing:

- Style
- Text
- Logic

Predict the result. Test it.

Curiosity never ends.

## AI Prompts (Chapter 30)

### Prompt 1 — Reflection

```
"Help me reflect on how my thinking has changed over the last 30 days."
```

### Prompt 2 — Confidence Builder

```
"Based on what I've learned, what evidence shows I'm no longer a
beginner?"
```

### Prompt 3 — Growth Planning

```
"Help me design a sustainable learning plan for the next 90 days."
```

### Prompt 4 — Identity Shift

```
"What does it mean to think like a web designer instead of a student?"
```

## Final Capstone Submission (Personal)

Document:

- Your final improvement
- Your live site URL
- What you're proud of
- What you'll build next

This is your **closing loop**.

## Final Reflection (Write This)

Answer honestly:

- Who were you on Day 1?
- Who are you now?
- What changed?

This matters more than any quiz.

## Book WrapUp — You Did It

You: Built real websites

Learned modern web fundamentals

Debugged, refactored, optimized

Deployed a live project

Became a selfdirected learner

You didn't just finish a book.

You changed how you learn.

## Final Message

You don't need permission to keep building.

You don't need another course to start.

You already know enough to grow.

Now go build something — and trust yourself.

End of Day 30. End of the book. Beginning of your journey.

# Appendix — Learning Resources, Reference & Next Steps

This appendix is designed to support you **after** you finish the book.

It is not meant to be memorized — it's meant to be **returned to**.

Use it as:

- A reference
- A confidence booster
- A guide for continued learning

## Core Web Design Concepts (Quick Reference)

### HTML (Structure)

HTML defines the **content and meaning** of a webpage.

Common elements:

- <h1>–<h6> — Headings
- <p> — Paragraphs
- <a> — Links
- <img> — Images
- <section> — Content grouping
- <header>, <main>, <footer> — Page structure

Key idea:

HTML answers *"What is this?"*

### CSS (Design)

CSS controls **layout, appearance, and visual hierarchy**.

Core concepts:

- Box model (margin, padding, border)
- Flexbox & layout basics
- Typography
- Color & contrast
- Responsive design fundamentals

Key idea:

CSS answers *"How should this look and feel?"*

### JavaScript (Behavior)

JavaScript controls **logic, interactivity, and dynamic content.**

Core concepts:

- Variables & data types
- Functions
- Events
- Arrays & objects
- DOM manipulation

Key idea:

JavaScript answers *"What should happen?"*

## Common Beginner Mistakes (and Why They're Normal)

You may still:

- Forget semicolons or brackets
- Misspell selectors
- Get null or undefined errors
- Feel like "nothing works"

This does **not** mean:

- You're bad at coding
- You didn't learn properly
- You should stop

It means:

You are doing real development work.

Mistakes are feedback.

## Debugging Cheat Sheet

When something doesn't work:

- Check the browser console
- Read the error message
- Identify the file and line number
- Add console.log() statements
- Verify assumptions
- Change one thing at a time

Never:

- Rewrite everything
- Panic
- Guess randomly

Debugging is a skill — and you are already practicing it.

## Vibe Learning Study Loop

Use this loop whenever you learn something new:

- Try — Write or change code
- Observe — What happened?
- Adjust — Change one thing
- Test — Did it improve?
- Reflect — What did you learn?

This loop works for:

- Web design
- Programming
- Any technical skill

# AI Prompts for Ongoing Learning

Use AI as a **learning partner**, not a shortcut.

## Explanation Prompts

- "Explain this code in simple terms."
- "Why does this work?"
- "What happens if I change this?"

## Debugging Prompts

- "Ask me questions to help debug this issue."
- "Explain this error message."
- "What are common mistakes here?"

## Growth Prompts

- "Suggest beginnerfriendly improvements to this project."
- "What should I learn next based on this code?"
- "How can I simplify this?"

Always review AI responses critically.

# Beginner Portfolio Checklist

Before sharing a project publicly, confirm:

- Clear purpose
- Clean layout
- Readable code
- Deployed URL
- Short description of what you built
- Explanation of what you learned

A portfolio is about **clarity**, not perfection.

# Appendix G — Suggested Next Topics (BeginnerSafe)

After this book, consider exploring:

- Responsive design & media queries
- Forms and input validation
- More JavaScript practice (arrays, objects, logic)
- Accessibility audits
- Small personal projects
- Code refactoring and cleanup

Avoid rushing into:

- Heavy frameworks
- Complex tooling
- Advanced build systems

Foundations compound.

# Learning Mindset Reminders

Keep these in mind as you continue:

- Confusion is not failure
- Slow progress is still progress
- Building beats watching
- Finishing beats perfect
- Confidence comes from repetition

You are allowed to:

- Experiment
- Make mistakes
- Learn at your pace

## About the Author

**Laurence Lars Svekis** is an educator, developer, and bestselling author who has taught **over 2 million students worldwide** how to code and build real projects.

Laurence specializes in making complex technical topics accessible through hands-on, beginner friendly teaching. His work focuses on helping learners build confidence by doing — not memorizing — and by understanding *how to learn*, not just what to learn.

This book reflects his belief that anyone can learn web design when the process is human, practical, and encouraging.

## Final Note to the Reader

If you reached this appendix, you finished the journey.

That matters.

You didn't just read a book — you built skills, habits, and confidence.

Now:

- Keep experimenting
- Keep building
- Keep trusting yourself

The web is open.

You belong here.

# Appendix — Glossary of Web Design & Development Terms

This glossary explains key terms **in simple language**, focused on *understanding*, not memorization.

## A

### Accessibility (A11y)

Designing websites so people with disabilities can use them (screen readers, keyboard navigation, color contrast, etc.).

### Array

A list of values stored in one variable in JavaScript.

```
["HTML", "CSS", "JavaScript"]
```

### Attribute

Extra information added to an HTML element.

```
<img src="image.jpg" alt="Description">
```

## B

### Block Element

An HTML element that takes up the full width (e.g., `<div>`, `<section>`, `<p>`).

### Browser

Software used to view websites (Chrome, Firefox, Safari, Edge).

## C

### CSS (Cascading Style Sheets)

Controls how a website looks (colors, layout, spacing, fonts).

### Class

A reusable label applied to HTML elements for styling or selection.

```
<div class="card"></div>
```

### Console

A browser tool used to view logs, errors, and debug JavaScript.

## D

### DOM (Document Object Model)

The browser's internal representation of your HTML that JavaScript can read and change.

### Deployment

Publishing your website so it's accessible on the internet.

## E

### Element

A single part of HTML, such as a paragraph, heading, or button.

### Event

An action that happens on a page (click, input, submit, load).

## F

### Function

A reusable block of JavaScript code that performs a task.

```
function greet() {
  console.log("Hello");
}
```

## H

### HTML (HyperText Markup Language)

Defines the structure and content of a webpage.

### Heading (*<h1>–<h6>*)

Used to organize content hierarchically.

## I

### ID

A unique identifier for an HTML element.

```
<section id="topics"></section>
```

### Input

A form element that accepts user data.

## J

### JavaScript

The programming language that adds logic and interactivity to websites.

## L

### Loop

A structure that repeats code (e.g., `for`, `forEach`).

### Layout

How elements are arranged on the page.

## M

### Media Query

CSS rules that apply styles based on screen size.

### Mutation

Changing data or content (often used with DOM updates).

## O

### Object

A JavaScript data structure that groups related values.

```
{ name: "Alex", level: "Beginner" }
```

## P

**Performance**

How fast and responsive a website feels.

**Property**

A key inside an object or a CSS rule.

## R

**Refactoring**

Improving code structure without changing what it does.

**Responsive Design**

Designing websites to work on all screen sizes.

## S

**Semantic HTML**

HTML elements that describe meaning, not appearance (`<header>`, `<main>`, `<section>`).

**Selector**

A way to target HTML elements using CSS or JavaScript.

## T

**Tag**

The name of an HTML element (`<p>`, `<div>`, `<img>`).

## U

**UI (User Interface)**

What the user sees and interacts with.

**UX (User Experience)**

How the site feels to use.

# V

### Variable

A container for storing data in JavaScript.

```
let count = 0;
```

# W

### Web Design

The practice of creating the structure, appearance, and behavior of websites.

# Appendix — Command & Reference Guide (Quick Lookup)

This appendix is a **practical cheat sheet** for common HTML, CSS, JavaScript, and browser tools used throughout the book.

## HTML Reference

### Basic Structure

```
<!DOCTYPE html>
<html>
<head>
  <title>Page Title</title>
</head>
<body>
</body>
</html>
```

### Common Elements

```
<h1>Heading</h1>
<p>Paragraph</p>
<a href="#">Link</a>
<img src="image.jpg" alt="Description">
<button>Click me</button>
```

### Semantic Layout

```
<header></header>
<nav></nav>
<main></main>
<section></section>
<footer></footer>
```

# CSS Reference

## Basic Syntax

```
selector {
  property: value;
}
```

## Common Properties

```
color
background
fontsize
margin
padding
display
flex
grid
```

## Flexbox Basics

```
display: flex;
justifycontent: center;
alignitems: center;
```

## Media Query

```
@media (maxwidth: 768px) {
  body {
    fontsize: 14px;
  }
}
```

# JavaScript Reference

## Variables

```
let name = "Alex";
const age = 25;
```

## Functions

```
function sayHello() {
  console.log("Hello");
}
```

### Arrays

```
let items = ["A", "B", "C"];
items.push("D");
```

### Objects

```
let user = {
  name: "Alex",
  role: "Beginner"
};
```

### Loops

```
for (let i = 0; i < items.length; i++) {}
items.forEach(item => {});
```

## DOM & Events

### Selecting Elements

```
document.querySelector("#id");
document.querySelector(".class");
```

### Creating Elements

```
document.createElement("div");
```

### Updating Content

```
element.textContent = "New text";
element.innerHTML = "<strong>Bold</strong>";
```

### Events

```
button.addEventListener("click", handleClick);
```

## Debugging & Tools

### Console Logging

```
console.log("Message");
```

### Common Errors

- ReferenceError
- TypeError
- SyntaxError

## Open DevTools

- Rightclick → Inspect
- F12
- Cmd + Option + I (Mac)

## Deployment Checklist (Quick)

`index.html` exists

File paths match exactly

No console errors

Site works locally

Site tested live

## Final Note on Reference Use

This appendix is **not a test**.

Use it when:

- You forget syntax
- You need reassurance
- You want to move forward confidently

Professional developers use references every day.

So can you.

# Modern Web Design Cheat Sheet

**HTML • CSS • JavaScript • DOM • Debugging**

*BeginnerFriendly Quick Reference*

## HTML — Structure

### Basic Page Template

```
<!DOCTYPE html>
<html lang="en">
<head>
  <meta charset="UTF8">
```

```
  <title>Page Title</title>
  <link rel="stylesheet" href="styles.css">
</head>
<body>
  <script src="script.js"></script>
</body>
</html>
```

### Common HTML Elements

```
<h1>Heading</h1>
<p>Paragraph</p>
<a href="#">Link</a>
<img src="img.jpg" alt="Description">
<button>Click</button>
<input type="text">
```

### Semantic Layout

```
<header></header>
<nav></nav>
<main></main>
<section></section>
<footer></footer>
```

**Rule:** Use semantic tags for meaning, not styling.

## CSS — Styling & Layout

### CSS Syntax

```
selector {
  property: value;
}
```

### Common CSS Properties

```
color
backgroundcolor
fontsize
margin
padding
border
```

```
width
height
display
```

### Box Model (Inside → Outside)

*content → padding → border → margin*

### Flexbox Essentials

```
display: flex;
justifycontent: center;
alignitems: center;
gap: 16px;
```

### Typography Defaults (Recommended)

```
body {
  fontsize: 16px;
  lineheight: 1.6;
}
```

### Media Query (Responsive)

```
@media (maxwidth: 768px) {
  body {
    fontsize: 14px;
  }
}
```

## JavaScript — Core Logic

### Variables

```
let count = 0;
const name = "Alex";
```

### Functions

```
function greet(name) {
  return "Hello " + name;
}
```

### Arrays

```
let items = ["HTML", "CSS", "JS"];
items.push("DOM");
items.length;
```

### Objects

```
let user = {
  name: "Alex",
  level: "Beginner"
};
```

### Loops

```
for (let i = 0; i < items.length; i++) {}
items.forEach(item => {
  console.log(item);
});
```

## DOM — Page Interaction

### Select Elements

```
document.querySelector("#id");
document.querySelector(".class");
```

### Create & Add Elements

```
const el = document.createElement("p");
el.textContent = "Hello";
document.body.appendChild(el)
```

### Update & Remove

```
element.textContent = "New text";
element.remove();
```

### Events

```
button.addEventListener("click", function () {
  console.log("Clicked");
});
```

## Debugging — Survival Kit

### Console Logging

```
console.log("Debug here");
```

### Common Errors

- ReferenceError → variable not defined
- TypeError → wrong data type or null
- SyntaxError → missing bracket or typo

### Debugging Checklist

Check console

Read error message

Check file + line number

Add `console.log()`

Fix one thing at a time

## Accessibility Quick Wins

Use semantic HTML

One `<h1>` per page

Buttons for actions (not `<div>`)

Labels for inputs

Keyboard navigation works

Visible focus styles

## Performance Basics

Cache DOM selectors

Don't rerender unnecessarily

Resize images before using

Keep CSS selectors simple

## Deployment Checklist

`index.html` exists

File names match exactly

No local file paths

No console errors

Site works live

## Vibe Learning Rules (Print These)

- Build first, perfect later
- Confusion = learning
- Small wins compound
- Finish > perfect
- Debugging is a skill

## AI Prompt Starters

- "Explain this code in simple terms"
- "Why doesn't this work?"
- "Ask me questions to debug this"
- "How can I simplify this code?"

## Final Reminder

Professional developers use cheat sheets. References are tools — not weakness.

Keep this nearby. Keep building.

# Index

# D

# T



# U



# W

www.ingramcontent.com/pod-product-compliance
Lightning Source LLC
LaVergne TN
LVHW060024210926
848481LV00013B/3784